20 Days Changed Everything

A Love Story: Moving Through Conscious Death to Afterlife Connection

Becki Koon

Praise For 20 Days Changed Everything

Becki's and Jack's love story and conscious death journey are a deeply healing experience to take part in, not only for those who currently are grieving the loss of a loved one but also for any of us that have tucked away old pain and sorrow. The compassion and love radiating from every page in this book have not only the potential of profound healing – it will also activate your own ability to hold a higher love for yourself and others.

Becki's and Jack's beautiful connection will also assist you who are open to anchor in the truth – that life never ends; it only shifts form. And when it does, we can remember our ability to be multidimensional and develop a new level of connection. They remind us that we are always connected, that we can communicate across the veil, and that love transcends everything.

Maria Marathon, Heart Connection Coach and Musical Intuitive, Heart Song Activation Guide

Founder of Heart Song

To birth a soul into human form on Earth is an act of love and sacrifice for that soul. But the ultimate sacrifice is to help birth a human loved one and companion, back home to spirit, and is the deepest form of unconditional love and sacrifice that exists.

Becki and Jack were destined to teach us, at the most intimate levels, the importance of understanding this process of birthing into death, and how they were able to work and move through it together. They show us that love is not separated between dimensions and how to continue to love through the veil. This is a story of devotion we all need to read because there will come a day we will all face this passage home, for ourselves or a loved one.

Jane Berryhill, M.S. Clinical Counseling, Biofeedback Therapist, Author (Forging the Flow, Emptying the Soul, Special and Then Some)

This love story transcending death is inspiring and uplifting on many levels. Most transparent is the depth and love in Becki and Jack's relationship. During Jack's conscious death process, Becki was able to rise above grief to make his transition as comfortable and dignified as possible. They continue to interact and work together in a completely different way: Jack from his side of the veil and Becki from her life in a physical form. Their story will be of great value as we all, one way or another, must face death and dying as we progress through human life. I feel honored and blessed to know both Becki and Jack. Their book allows many others to know them as well.

Adele Lewis, Animal Communicator, former Wildlife Rehabilitator, Author (Listening to Animals by Adele Lewis Coon)

This book is like a drink of water to a thirsty soul. We are facing an unprecedented time in the history of the planet. People are leaving the Earth unexpectedly and at an alarming rate due to many factors. The majority of the people are leaving in traumatic circumstances. Death and the dying process can be beautiful transitions when tended with awareness and care.

Becki's book follows the steps she took with her partner, Jack, as they faced his death. Her shared experience has helped me work with others at the doorway of death. I knew what to do to comfort them as a direct result of her book and conversations. Most people don't walk with death easily but this book puts you at ease with approaching death as a friend.

Terry Du Beau, Head Start Teacher for Makah Tribe in Northwest Washington

This beautifully poignant love story is a wonderful reminder that love does not end with this life experience. Our experiences together continue beyond what we realize here in this limited space and time.

Like love, we continue to grow, expand, experience, and interact in wonderful ways, ever-evolving, as individuals and as one. Our souls sing and dance in a beautiful rhythm and melody of love, light, and joy through one earthly experience after another and beyond. Our souls dancing and playing like fall leaves in the gusty breeze, free flowing through the dance of time and space with ease and grace. This book is a touching reminder of that dance and the true depths of love and connection that we share in our 3D humanness and in the expansion of our soul essence within all that is. It is a reminder of true self essence, hope, and love unending.

Sherry Quarnstrom, CCHT, Intuitive Guide and Personal Empowerment Coach, Author (Shine)

Dedication

To my beloved Jack and our never-ending dance of love and soul connection.

Table of Contents

Foreword

"Where there is Love, there is Life"

Mahatma Gandhi

While studying to be a nurse before becoming a Hospice RN, I was told "Death is not personal. If we are born, we will die." That statement, as true as it is…is not true.

Love guides and carries us through our lifetime. We find Love in our God, in the beauty of Nature, in our friends and family, in service to others, and in our relationships. When we cry out in need, the Divine shows up to help us.

"What took place this day forever changed me. I had no idea how much courage I had within until I witnessed it. I had no idea of the depths to which love can go until I experienced it. I had no idea of the vastness of the human heart until I lived it". (Becki)

Love transcends everything, so why not Death?

This is a journey of Becki and Jack who loved each other to death and then continued in a life of Love together. They traveled into the depth of Love, in pain and sorrow, loss and grief, with a mutual desire to explore "Life after Death".

Their story is one of the extraordinary connections between two people, creating the courage to Live and Love each other in both worlds.

They meet again and again in the opening of a rare window of Light...a gateway of Divine Love, with Jack and Becki together.

This is their journey, experienced moment to moment.

For them, Death is personal and so is Life.

Becki and Jack give hope to us all, of a continuing Love together, beyond Death into Light.

" Life and Death are One, as the river and the sea are One"

Kahlil Gibran

Christina Oss LaBang

Hospice RN and Author

'ANDEANsolrocks: Pathway of Light'

Preface

With great humility and gratitude, I gift this book to the world. Its conception came from a dying man's wish, my beloved, the man I consider my soul mate. For many years, Jack nudged me to write the unformed book I felt inside and thought I was to write. Sadly, the book you are reading only came into existence with his diagnosis of terminal cancer and his conscious death passage 20 days later.

He knew this book, born of our loss, would take both of us on a journey of discovery into the realm of conscious death and, perhaps, afterlife connection. We wondered if it was possible for our love to transcend the boundaries between the land of human life and spirit life. We were hopeful.

So, I wrote to him during our process and about my expanded reality after he left, writings often magical and mysterious but always born of a divine love connection between us.

He was right. We are still on a journey together. We share afterlife communication, expansion, and a love that never dies, only transforms, continuing to evolve.

Twenty Days Changed Everything is our book, a book of hope, gestated over a year, and birthed into a world that can benefit from the awareness of life after life. Jack and I want readers to know we need not fear our future after the death passage. Our loved ones are near. It is our desire this book lessens fear and opens the door to expanded consciousness, the reality of afterlife connection, and love transcending all. Love is the vibration of the divine universe. This book is our gift of love to everyone.

Becki and Jack

Step Stone Studio, 2020

Introduction

Oh God, how it hurts, especially at night; the deafening silence of being alone almost unbearable, my love. The seconds seem to warp, time moves in desolate slow motion, I am in isolation. I can't hold back the tears that erupt from the center of my being like a volcano with such force my breath is snatched away, lost in an eruption of grief. I remind myself you are near, in the energetic field surrounding me and, at the same time, I curse you are gone. My memory of you is a precious gem I squeeze with a grip that seems to strangle the moment. Please, please, Jack, hold me. Let me feel you, your arms around me once again, your hands caressing my skin with the magic you carry, your breath gently washing away my pain.

I sob for several minutes, allowing the tears to flow through me, allowing myself to feel the heartache of your physical death. My nose plugs, my eyes swell, and I blow grief into the tissue I hold in my hands. Momentarily the energy moves out of my body, allowing a deep inhale of breath, filling my lungs with life. Yes, I am still here, alone in the silence of our room.

I begin to work with my breath, feeling my heart even though it hurts. I have the tools. I know what to do; it is what I teach others. Heart-focused breathing and finding the higher vibrational emotions of compassion, gratitude, appreciation, and love have saved me since we were told your body would not survive cancer. The twenty-day conscious death process we experienced was full of intensity, and we practiced focused breathing whenever we remembered, sharing as much love as was humanly possible.

Tonight, I find my breath once again, slowly moving from overwhelming sadness to peace. My head hurts, but I am navigating another human moment of missing your physical presence. Gratitude is my reward as I calm and allow myself to settle into the bed, cuddling the body pillow a friend of ours gifted me after you left.

As I continue to breathe, my body relaxes, my mind quiets, and I remember how to connect with you. I begin to feel into my body, and I ask divine Source, my guides, angels, and you to help me move this energy through. I ask you to come close, to hold me while the waves of emotions dissipate.

Then it happens. I sense the now-familiar cool sensation of your soul behind me, holding me. I allow my higher awareness to step into the multi-dimensional realm of connection. The veil has thinned, and I am fully aware of your presence. I can almost physically feel your touch through the cool vibration that envelops me. I acknowledge you and immediately experience a visceral response. I hear you say, "I am here, my love. Breathe into me!" I feel a small, cool tickle of energy swirling on my forehead, down my face, then traveling down my neck and shoulder.

My grief melts away in the precious recognition you are absolutely with me, holding me, caressing me, and my heart finds a gracious peace. I thank you, my love, for helping assuage the challenge I face without you. You have shared you are closer to me now than even in life. What a blessing it is to have you in this way, our connection not finished; we are finding a new way of being beyond conscious thought.

As I ease into your energetic embrace, I am grateful for everything we shared, everything we share now, and everything the future holds. Love never dies, and the more I step into this vibrational insight, the more I feel my life expand. I can do this. I am surviving the waves of emotion, no matter how hard they crash onto my internal shores.

Thank you, my love. I can now fall into a restful sleep, feeling your never-ending love encircling me.

Jack and I had 12 wonderful years together in our physical life, our coming together a tale of two souls deeply entwined from the beginning, aware of a previous soul connection. We loved our life together. We shared this gift of life, the ability to find the higher-level emotions of joy, compassion, gratitude, love, appreciation, and courage in the face of even the most challenging situations. Our everyday activity was full of spiritual awakening, exploration, and diving into the esoteric nature of living on this planet we likened to the tick-tock of the third-dimensional (3D) matrix. Vibrational frequency was part of our normal radar, both of us empathic and sensitive to the energetic field surrounding us. We were steeped in soul remembering. And we loved Earth; crystals and stones surrounded our living space. Our business was called Step Stone for a reason. We were excited to be starting a whole new trajectory in business together. Life was great!

And then...

The most daunting task we experienced together was Jack's death process. I don't believe many people knowingly choose conscious death, but when faced with the irrefutable truth of his cancer-filled body, we accepted the journey with grace and courage. Gratitude came in waves as the moments carried a sacred energy we both cherished while his body continued to let go, to shut down to life as we had known it.

This book is a love story, a journey of immeasurable soul connection, of love that walks you through the conscious death passage of my husband, Jack, into the amazing, magical, and often surreal world of afterlife connection. I am one of the fortunate. I was blessed to be able to say goodbye, to hold him in my arms. I felt the last breath leave his body, no breath to follow, just complete stillness, a quiet, heart-wrenching peace filling the space that was his living body just seconds before.

What is conscious death? I know the term has been used by many but my definition is based on first-hand experience, my personal definition may or may not be the same as what others have shared. For us, when Jack accepted his journey

Introduction

to death's gate, we both stepped into active participation with the process of letting go: letting go of his life here, his body, our future, his trauma, his possessions, letting go of each other in the physical realm. The one thing we never let go of was our undying love, holding onto it tightly through all challenges.

We shaped his walk into the next expression, knowing full well his life force was not ending but transforming into soul, his essence into the next version of expression. We chose to work together as a team, making his passage become the best possible outcome for him in his last days. We worked diligently to help him release the earthly plane despite how gut-wrenching it was at times. Many have written about love like ours, a love that transcends the physical expression, moving into divine soul expression. We performed conscious death.

A large portion of Part 1 of the book was written as a love letter to Jack while we were experiencing the 20-day journey from diagnosis to death. I wrote it as a diary each day and read the entries to him several times along the way. I read the final entry to him after his passage, my way to honor him and what we had both experienced, my last love letter to Jack, spoken to his form from a heart filled with anguish for me and complete joy for him.

After each diary entry, I share the backstory of how we accomplished the day, what our thoughts were, tasks we performed to assist us in moving forward along the journey. It is my hope somewhere in these pages, readers find useful tools, ideas that resonate with them. I have no claim to any process nor do I feel expert in any one technique. It is a profoundly personal exposure of our life that can help those going through the process of letting go of life as we know it on the planet. We all experience the death passage; whether it be of loved ones or ourselves, it is inevitable. I want all to know this book is a heartfelt walk into love, love for Jack, love for me, and love for all those actively walking the death transition. The experience changes a person. I am grateful for having walked with my love into life after life.

What unfolded after Jack's transformation from bodily life to spirit life is the real adventure Jack and I want to share, a testament to life after life, our afterlife connection.

Part 2 of the book begins in October, the first month after Jack passed. These chapters are laid out as a diary of the nine months following his body leaving. They outline the process of afterlife connection we began to experience and how I moved through grief into trust with the events of psychic opening and mediumship as it unfolded along the way. Synchronicity and magic played a big part in the expanded awareness that was to become my new life.

My love no longer has life here, but I see him, feel his loving presence, speak with him, receive messages from him. The deep spiritual connection we shared has not disappeared; it has transformed, taken on a new life, a new identity, one of eternal, undying love. Does that mean I am not experiencing grief and sadness? Not at all! I find myself in moments that catch my breath, stop me in my tracks, tears always ready to erupt and fall. And yet, I celebrate that I behold him in his soul expression, layered with so much love, so much light, so much bliss I find myself having no fear of joining him, any fear of death now gone from my psyche.

What I know–physical death is not the end. It is a passing from one form into the next, and our loved ones are always near. If we choose to become aware, we can all learn how to connect. Jack is in constant communication with me now, and I am learning to let go of any doubts, to allow and trust this new form of relationship with him. The veil between our dimensions is becoming transparent.

At the end of each chapter is a channeled message from Jack. He is thrilled to share this information with all of us.

We have inside of us an enormous capacity for evolution, growth, and resiliency to change, no matter how uncomfortable the circumstances. When we bypass the thinking-brain and move into our heart-brain, we find the courage to take a chance, to expand into a state of Being previously unknown to us. We find we are held with a pearl of divine wisdom that radiates a secure blanket of comfort as we navigate the next step and the next step and the next step.

We are all souls living in this remarkable human form that falls down and gets back up, experiences heartbreak and loves again, feels paralyzed by fear and finds a way to move forward or at least break through the challenges. Those who are reading this book are likely to understand love transcends all, the soul inside lives on. While in human form, we are warriors of light, lighting the way for others to see, to follow, and to find hope while navigating the trials and tribulations which are expressions of the beautiful human condition.

I am writing with the premise readers have a basic understanding of energy concepts such as, our 7-energy center chakra system and the auric energy field surrounding our bodies. There are numerous resources available regarding the research of the energy fields of the human body and other spiritual ideas. I encourage those who feel pulled to learn more to dive further into energetic and spiritual concepts. My goal is merely to share a personal journey, to be the storyteller of a wondrous, undying love between two souls, me and Jack.

In the conclusion, I offer final words of hope and a few resources I found useful in the process of supporting my love in his conscious death passage.

Join me on this journey into finding courageous heart through love, loss, and afterlife connection. May this book be the salve to help you and others walk the hard yet inevitable journey through deaths passage into the afterlife wonder.

Part 1 - 20 Days to Physical Death

The infinity inside of me

That part of me that is the God Force

Loves and respects this human evolution of mine.

It loves and respects where I find myself,

My current circumstances.

So I will do the same,

Even though the circumstances of my life

May be less than best,

All these things are a part of my growth.

I will transcend and go beyond them.

My Love Jack's Words

2007

September 4, 2019

How do I begin to say goodbye to you, my love? Cancer is a common word we hear every day, often many times in a day. Yet, when you hear that word in an emergency room from the attending physician, the name somehow takes on a different and surreal meaning. I know, as they wheel you away for the CT scan, your life and mine will be forever changed. Somehow, I know the answer to come and yet I smile and brightly say, "See you in just a few minutes, my love."

You come back into the ER, and we joke amidst the smell of antiseptics and the beeping of monitors. Those few minutes seem to drag, and time morphs into its own slow dance. "I love you. Maybe they will give you a prescription to will help your pneumonia," I say in encouragement.

The doctor enters slowly and sits down. I lovingly look at you as you smile and ask her, "What's the good news?" Her eyes drop, she shakes her head and says, "It's not good news. A nine-centimeter malignant tumor has taken residence in the right lung, and the cancer has metastasized into the liver, kidneys, lymph nodes, and probably many other organs." I look at you, feeling stunned, full of dread mixed with compassion, but not surprised. You look at me as you say to the doctor, "Well, this must be why I have been coughing up blood and feeling so sick. Makes sense." You then look over to the doctor

2

and ask her what the prognosis for time is. "A few days?" you joke and smile.

She looks you squarely in the eyes while fighting back her tears and says solemnly, "Perhaps a couple of months."

Wow! My heart skips, beats rapidly. My skin immediately flushes, my cheeks burning. Okay then, options. The doctor says, "You can stay here in the hospital, speak to an oncologist, and run through a battery of tests to determine the exact type of cancer and what other organs are affected. Treatment might buy you another couple of months, but you need to consider your quality of life during that time. No one else can make these decisions for you." She leaves us alone to digest what we just heard.

I look at you with love; we stare into each other's eyes for a long, heartfelt moment, time standing still, and finally you say, "I am going home. You with me on this, my love?"

With my heart breaking open, feeling exposed and raw, I say, "Of course I am!"

We go home with medications to help ease your high level of discomfort from coughing and pain. We talk about many things but you have something extremely important to share with me. You tell me you recognize the doctor, not from this life, but from before you came to this planet, from before our human life realm. When you looked into her eyes, you

3

knew she had chosen to be the light being who would share this news with you. The two of you had a contract of sorts; this event was a planned potential in your life. You know all this with every fiber of your being.

We talk about life path journeys. We talk about how we believe a soul can have many potential exit points along life's timeline, but we are hopeful your journey is one of miraculous healing. You encourage me by being positive and upbeat, despite your shortness of breath and increasingly severe pain.

The News

And so we began what was to be our 20-day vigil.

How were we able to receive the information about his terminal cancer with a high level of grace, awareness, and acceptance? Notice I did not say we weren't shocked, stunned, and thrown into a reality that shook us to the core. But in hearing the news, the soul aspect in both of us knew the journey ahead, neither of us denying the truth of the diagnosis.

When Jack and I found each other 12 years earlier, we experienced a soul recognition, something we could not explain but deeply felt. I believe many people have looked at someone and sensed they somehow knew them with no recollection of meeting in this life. Many have had a magnetic draw to another person they cannot explain but it is so strong it cannot be denied. This was our meeting: a recognition of knowing each other from before this life, in another time, in another reality.

We knew we were soul partners, not only in this life but in relation to divine partnership. We believed we had some form of agreement forged before entering this life, a contract of sorts to meet at this time, to come together and grow into our combined spiritual nature. Exploring esoteric and metaphysical principles was a constant topic of discussion in our world and we explored energy dynamics as it related to our intuitive awareness.

We came to understand both of us were natural empaths; the energy surrounding us and other people had a strong and palpable impact on us. Jack was a highly sensitive and philosophical man who played his life out through the creation of beautiful music, the guitar being his instrument of choice. Music soothed his tattered soul and he transformed his challenges through the creation of heartfelt melodies. I would watch him transfixed by music, by beautiful melody, tears streaming down his face from the sound penetrating his soul.

He would often become overwhelmed by what he sensed when we were out and about in town. Sometimes he would ask me to go into a store by myself because he knew he did not have the internal energy reserve to field all the psychic information and chaotic energy bombarding him.

The positive side of having this type of sensitivity is a keen awareness of spiritual matters, an understanding of the subtle realm surrounding all of us. This led to diving deep into connection to soul, an unwavering knowledge that this life experience is only one small part of who we really are. When we met, Jack had an awakening that led him to study aspects of why he was here, who he really was, and the temporal nature of his body, a knowing that time is an illusion to the eternal nature of being.

We were blessed with a divine love growing from a recognition that we chose to come together to travel the road of love partnership, no matter how challenging. Unwavering love meant we allowed each other the freedom of choice, stepping into compassion and unconditional love from trust in each other, in the love we shared. We often told each other that, if this partnership ever stopped working for one of us, it was okay to separate, love binding us beyond the physical togetherness, unconditioned by need.

That depth of love was present and strong between us when my partner, with a terminal cancer diagnosis, looked at me and said, "I am going home. You with me in this, my love?"

Even though we were both surprised to hear the diagnosis of cancer, Jack knew his journey; there was no denying what he had been feeling inside, how his body was reacting and responding to a rapidly growing and aggressive cancer. Do I fully understand how he was able to come to terms with his diagnosis so quickly? No, but I do know his connection to his higher self, the soul existing inside his body, was so strong that he was not horrified by the news; a little shocked

6

but not in any fear of life and death hanging in balance on the tightrope of his reality. He rested in knowing he is an eternal being in a third-dimensional form, having a momentary experience in physical form before going back home.

We both understood the ways of the spiritual warrior, those souls who come to this planet to live through, rise above and conquer a variety of challenges, to do business with the egoic structure of the limited mind, and to introduce soul expansion and freedom while navigating the density of the human form. We were prepared to step into the life and death arena, no matter what came to be. We were ready to take up the swords of loving compassion and eternal life truth as our weapons.

Besides, we knew miracles happen all the time and miraculous healings take place.

September 5, 2019

*We spend the day together alone in a state of shock.
I call into work and excuse myself, so I can just be
with you. We decide not to talk to anyone; we need
time to absorb this new reality first. You get a little
relief from the cough medicine, but you are still
coughing up blood. We talk about miracles. We both
know they happen, they are real, and there is no
reason you can't be one of them, my love. You talk to
your body and cellular structure while we hold each
other, understanding that time is now even more
precious to us than it always has been. Our journey
together is one of self-discovery and exploration into
the spiritual essence of who we are: always asking
the big questions, recognizing that time is relative, a
perception of our current reality, a key to how we live
and honor our love connection.*

*My son happens to be going through town, so he
stops by for a quick hello. It is awkward and he does
not know what to say to you, my love; he knows this
may be the last time he sees you. You share some of
your wisdom with him because his journey is
challenging, much like yours has been. He does love
you, both of you sharing a unique connection. My son
is how we initially met, and he was again the catalyst
when we became a couple. He has an appointment in
town, so he tells you goodbye. He holds me tight
when I walk him to the door. It is healing for me to
feel his hug, his loving support. He tells me how*

much he loves me and that it will all be okay, no matter how it turns out. I know he is right.

We have some business to complete, so we head to Missoula after my son leaves. A new Sony large screen TV was just delivered to us two weeks ago. We had planned to show spiritual movies through our business, but that dream is now blasted into a reality we did not expect. We have not even unpacked the box yet; it is in the room just as they delivered it. You are clear the financed TV is not a burden you want me to have, so we head to the store to ask them to work with us. When you share with the young manager how our lives have changed, that you have been given a 2-month window for survival and do not want to leave me with the added debt, he is amazed. He is in awe of your composure, your compassion for how hard it hit him, for the deep love and concern for me that you shared with him. You touch this young man's heart and, without hesitation and at no expense to us, he vows to arrange a delivery pick-up. They are kind and understanding.

To honor our time together, we decide to go to one of your favorite restaurants for dinner before heading home. As we eat our meal, your cough starts to well up. You hold your self-control beautifully, and your biggest concern is to avoid worrying or disturbing the other patrons in the restaurant. I am touched by your compassion for others, even now. By the time we head out to the car, you cough again, and we wait until you regain your breath before we start the drive home. You tell me you are aware this is the last time we will eat out together because you do not want to become a spectacle in front of others. "Of course, this is just until you get better, right, honey?" I say.

Integration

My heart was extremely heavy with the news the doctor shared and yet, amidst all the trauma engulfing us, I found a path into heart. How did we begin to integrate the shock of the news? We gave ourselves into each other's divine love as much as possible. We held each other tight. We cried as our embrace took on a new meaning, feeling our bodies entwined and energetically connected in the now moments, recognizing this too shall pass. I never questioned or second-guessed his decision to come home. I supported him 100% even though I did not know the intensity of spiritual courage my decision would call forth.

I was supposed to work at my part-time job but called in sick, not ready to talk to anyone. I needed time to absorb the news; we needed time alone and yet the impromptu visit from my son added salve to my open-heart wound. My son held me tight while I trembled in his arms as we embraced when he said goodbye. His words of support added some stability to my shaky resolve and yet the intuitive part of me knew it would be the last time he would see Jack alive.

Jack and I had certain errands to run, the urgency of time now pressing our reality into taking care of business. I was blown away to witness Jack's self-composure, his concern for me and others with whom he interacted during our day. I was witness to and inspired by his spiritual warrior in action. He carried his empathy for others in the open, not afraid to be a man who shared his deep emotional connection regarding the reality of terminal cancer.

His compassion for other people had always drawn me into a state of gratitude for this man who could openly show gentleness and concern, his empathy and awareness of others' feelings driving his nurturing qualities. Many men are conditioned to believe this kind of display is weak, unmanly, and yet this type of man shows an act of courage beyond stereotypes, an acceptance of the feminine aspects within himself. As humans, we all carry energetic properties of male and female, qualities of both that, when balanced, provide a complete human expression.

In the 12 years we spent together, Jack and I often meditated to uplift ourselves and bring us into higher-awareness states. We loved to meditate together, go on guided journeys, and then share what our adventures yielded. Now, meditation was a tool we used to calm our nerves as the uncertain future raised its head to be seen and felt.

As a licensed HeartMath Coach, I teach breathing techniques to help others during times of stress. I love how simple the techniques are and I readily used them to calm my racing thoughts while watching Jack's breath, which became even more painful, labored. He could no longer take a deep breath but he did focus on breathing through his heart, tapping into his divine wisdom, while he sought counsel from his higher consciousness, his light-being soul.

As a Reiki Master, I worked with that healing energy, sending waves of peace to Jack's expanding discomfort and to my emotional stability. Reiki is a light-touch, divine healing energy that directs itself through the experienced practitioner, a conduit in the electromagnetic field surrounding the body. People often feel deep relaxation, stress reduction, and pain relief, all amplified when combined with relaxing music, essential oils, and focused breathing. I was practicing this on both of us as we navigated our changing world.

We talked about the miracle of the human body and how healing can take place miraculously. Jack spoke to his cells and his body, encouraging them to heal. We held hope in our arms like a warm blanket as we cuddled each other when the moments allowed.

September 6, 2019

We are hopeful but understand that your life is on the line.

You encourage me to work with my clients who are scheduled today so my Reiki/Coaching business can continue moving forward. Our shop, Step Stone, has been open for almost a year now. You are so proud of my work and service in the world. You insist that you want me to conduct the scheduled appointments if I am feeling up to it,.

I find within me the strength to see those clients and am grateful for the distraction. The last couple of days have been filled with the shock of the news, our lives turned upside down, life and death a topic of discussion in the most intimate ways. I find gratitude for the Reiki sessions that are wonderfully healing for my clients and give me much needed loving and healing energy through being the conduit in service to others.

Life Does Not Stop

Somewhere within me I was able to find the resolve to move forward with Jack's request that I keep my Reiki and Coaching clients who were already booked that day. I was feeling unsteady, not yet ready to share this news publicly. I questioned my ability to be in service to others in a professional manner when my reality was being shaken to the core, my heart aching from it all.

But Jack knew the healing work was beneficial for me and would add some normalcy, so this is how I navigated my day:

> I sat in my reception center and took a few moments to breathe. I focused on my heart and asked my higher awareness and spiritual team of guides to assist me in being of the highest service to those under my care. I visualized my body feeling peace and ease as I kept breathing into the moment, feeling my breath move in and out of my body. By the time my first client came to the Wellness Center, my mind was calm and being ready.

I was able to focus on my clients fully and completely. It was as if part of my grief-filled reality had been set aside for a little while and it felt almost normal to be doing the work I love.

Between sessions, I checked on Jack, making sure he was as comfortable as possible. What a blessing it was to be living right next to our business! The realization that we were in the perfect location to be going through this journey together was present and I found gratitude in those moments of closeness to both him and my healing work.

By the last session of the day, I noticed my weakening armor. It was a Reiki session, and while I always ask my ego mind to step aside and allow Spirit to move through me, this time it was imperative that Spirit guide my hands. I was able to sense my sadness while feeling the love of my higher self coaching me through the session. I was in a state of multidimensional awareness, clearly setting aside my pain, allowing my guides to hold me. The true testament to my allowing Spirit to do the work was when my client reported she had a sensational session. She was so appreciative and felt the relief she had been seeking, none the wiser to my current scenario.

We often forget we can call on Spirit, our higher self, our guides, angels, our family of light. It does not matter what labels we use for these beings; they are the higher energies who are always present to assist us. Jack and I both carried an awareness of that connection and we often marveled at our ability to step into altered states of reality with the support of our team of light beings.

When I finished the day, I returned to the inner room to be with Jack, in full recognition that my spirit team had been holding me, healing me, assisting me in diverting my worry while I gave of myself in service to others. Then I collapsed into Jack's arms for the rest of the night.

Jack had found a YouTube channel that played meditative music behind a backdrop of beautiful landscape scenes from around the planet. We had already set up the bed in the music recording studio, his favorite room. The bed faced the artistic brick and mortar wall where his guitars hung and we added a temporary stand with a smart TV so we could watch movies together since he was becoming more and more bedridden from weakness and fatigue. The studio became our safe haven.

15

As I lay in his arms, we listened and watched the beautiful earth, in awe of this planet and all we hold dear.

September 7, 2019

You are concerned about leaving me in a financial mess, debt from our new business venture still outstanding. You decide to call a friend to ask whether he is interested in buying two of your most treasured guitars. They have great value, and before you offer them to an online selling platform, you want to make sure he has the first option of purchase. Another time and under different circumstances, you would have gifted those instruments to him, but time is not our ally right now, and your most significant stress is our debt load. Your friend does not hesitate to say yes. He wants to have a piece of your essence. "And besides," he says, "when you get better, you can have them back! If I buy these guitars, it will help relieve some of your stress, and you can then focus on healing!"

You are relieved, yet I see a deep regret in your eyes, a sadness that you are even having that conversation with him.

You urge me to go to a dear friend's wedding today. I am hesitant as I do not want to seem distracted at her wedding and am uncomfortable leaving you. Yet you are so sure you want me to go and have fun that I find resolve within to say I will go. We have shared news of the cancer with only the closest family and friends. I honor your wishes to keep it under wraps. Your best friend, Jozy, is coming to be with you, so I am relieved you are not alone, my love. My girlfriend

17

is my emotional support while attending, and we go and honor the expression of love so beautifully celebrated at the wedding. Despite feeling nauseous the last several days, I enjoy the lovely dinner served to guests and am happy to find moments of joy with friends and family, no one but my girlfriend the wiser.

Distractions

Neither of us got much sleep that night. Our conversations were full of urgency as we discussed life and death, healing and transition, miracles and magic. We were both firm believers in the body's natural ability to heal. Jack and I had read and followed people like Dr. Joe Dispenza and Dr. Bruce Lipton. We had taken courses in healing and personally experienced magical events that had no logical explanation. Therefore, we did what we did best: we talked the night away and into the next day.

Jack's biggest concern at that time was leaving me in a financial bind. We had no preparations in place for this type of event; living life moment to moment was a gift we shared, but it suddenly felt like short-sightedness on our part. We had invested in opening our business, Step Stone, and the debt owed weighted heavily on Jack's mind and heart. He felt as though he had made some poor decisions in light of what our future looked like in that Now moment. The possessions of most value to Jack were his instruments and, being high-end instruments, they held their worth. His friend jumped at the chance to help us, believing if Jack's financial concerns were lifted, beating cancer would be easier to achieve.

I remained hopeful, stepped into a vibrational field supporting healing, and was ready to spend every moment with Jack when he suggested I go to the wedding that had been on my calendar for months. I was not prepared to leave his side but when Jozy came by and said he would stay with Jack. I felt better, knowing he would be in good hands.

I shared the news of Jack's illness with a dear friend who was going and asked her to be my support at the wedding celebration. I knew she had my back. She drove us there; in case things got shaky, we agreed on a signal I could give her meaning I needed to head home. I did not want anyone else to sense my anxiety. The wedding was a beautiful event and I navigated the evening with grace and consciousness.

I was in a form of prayer much of the time and was grateful for the delightful banquet they shared with guests. It was the first full meal I had been able to stomach since receiving the news. I felt such love and joy between the bride and groom, and from a place deep within my soul, I was able to share with them the awe-inspiring power of love, of sharing a deep and abiding soul connection that could be honored and cherished always, never taken for granted. As I spoke the words, my soul was crying from understanding how temporary life can be, how fragile the ground of terminal illness.

I texted Jack to make sure all was well and he responded he just wanted me to enjoy my time with family and friends. As I gazed at the beautiful sunset, I took a picture to send him. He had such a complete connection with nature, the clouds, skies, trees, birds, and animals. I knew the photo would make him smile for a moment.

Nature was one way we stayed connected to each other, often sharing stories and photos during our day. Jack had a unique gift in noticing the small world, the magic in the mundane. I developed a more in-depth cognizance of nature because of his influence.

September 8, 2019

Today we choose to be together, discussing the hard, life-altering realities bearing down on us, weighing heavily on our hearts. We know we have to make contact with a few key people.

We visit with our landlords from whom we rent both business and apartment space. They have become like family and were so excited to have us come back to rent from them after being away for five years. They are elderly, and their vision was that you would be around to assist with the building maintenance and help in the event they needed extra support. You are like a son to them. When we tell them the news, they are stunned. Our landlord is 91 and, with tear-choked voice, he cries, "It should be me, not you! I have lived a long, good life; you are so young with so much to live for. It should be me!" He is shaken to his core and I witness you comforting him. You reassure him, showing gentle love and compassion. You are concerned this will take a toll on him, his health. You are uplifting and tell them you can heal from this if anyone can.

Your friend comes for your favorite guitars. It is heartbreaking for me to witness you letting go of a piece of your soul, knowing how much music is a part of you. You have managed and healed your pain through he years by creating beautiful music, transforming hardship into the magic that moves the heart of all those fortunate enough to hear you play.

21

Those two instruments carry your soul signature, your musical essence, and we silently watch them leave your studio tonight. I see part of you die a little more at that moment. I watch the tears well in your eyes as you thank your friend for helping us in our time of need. You also feel some relief, my love, knowing we could take care of some upcoming expenses we were otherwise unable to meet.

Sharing the News

Reality sank in and we knew some key people needed to be informed of our situation. We honored ourselves first and took the time we needed to absorb this new life that had been thrust upon us. News like cancer and terminal illness throws all aspects of life off center and we felt it necessary to allow ourselves time to find a form of integrated steadiness as a couple. We knew those aspects of our well-being had been impacted and it was essential to find a state of balance, even if that balance was off-kilter.

This news impacts the physical body. My symptoms were nausea, hot flushes, heart palpitations, and loss of appetite. They paled compared to what Jack was suffering so, I was not even phased by my body adjusting to the news. I understood the temporary nature of this expression; I could accept and deal with what my body was manifesting. Jack, on the other hand, was going down a much different road, his destination uncertain.

Emotional well-being is impacted. My heartache and grief with the news were real, tangible, yet my awareness about our spiritual love connection was even more vital. That knowledge carried me while I allowed the tears and shock to move through my body. Jack stepped into full acceptance but also allowed himself to have moments of tears.

It certainly affects our mental state. Fatigue had set in for both of us. Jack had been coughing through the night for about a month before we found out about cancer so we were both running on fumes. I had to work at staying clear-headed, focused on the task at hand, but it was as if a higher aspect of myself stepped up to the plate and said, "It's my turn to bat so you can take care of the needs of the guy on the bench." I was grateful for the ability to stay mentally alert. Jack was in a hyper-focused state, dealing with his ever-changing physical environment. I had to continually let go of worry, refocusing my mind on the moment-to-moment tasks at hand.

Sudden, life-threatening news can even impact the spiritual state, but this area in our lives remained solid, unwavering. I have a strong faith in my higher soul, knowing I have a greater purpose. Now more than ever, I called on that higher insight to guide me. Jack was continuously calling in his spiritual team, asking for spiritual ammunition to fight his battle. He knew his teammates had his back no matter what the outcome of the game.

Having balanced those aspects of impact in our own ways, Jack and I were ready to share the news with others. Only a handful of people had been told. We held a strong energetic field of compassion as we informed other family and friends, knowing how those who cared for us would be affected by this development. We wanted to hold them in love.

That strong energy field was how Jack held the courage to watch a part of his life walk out the door, the guitars that were an extension of his essence. I silently cried my loss as I too was saying goodbye; I had spent hours listening to those instruments when Jack poured his heart out for me in musical love. I often marveled while watching him hold the guitars because he showed such a reverence for them, caressing them with a recognition of the soul they carried within their form. Jack told me they each have a unique personality. I often joked with him about watching him make love to the guitar as he played. It was beautiful to witness and I knew that a special part of our lives was gone.

September 9, 2019

We schedule an emergency appointment with our family nurse practitioner (FNP), our primary caregiver. She is the only person you trust and will see. We have a good and positive appointment with her, but you struggle to breathe, coughing up blood toward the end of the visit. You marvel at the beautiful stones in her consulting room and send pictures of the giant selenite wands to your best friend, Jozy. We get a plan in place, and she gifts us with a book by Bernie Siegel called Love, Medicine, and Miracles. *We are still holding a vision of hope that you have the strength of healing. We introduce a new medication for your cough and painful hiccups, which now occur frequently. We also set up an appointment with a Medical Intuitive to get to the cancer's root energetic cause. We believe she can give us some guidance about what your body needs to heal on an energetic and emotional level to make you comfortable.*

Later at home, as I read aloud the first chapter of the book we were gifted, you stop me. "I can't do this right now. I am not one of the exceptional people he writes about. I have never been one of the exceptional people. My life was not orchestrated that way," you say. I respond, "I don't see it that way, my love. You have lived an amazing life and touched so many people by how you have shared your talents, knowledge, and wisdom, not only musically but also

with your spiritual journey, self-discovery, and
connection to nature. I don't think you realize how
many lives you have impacted or how many people
care for you. You are exceptional in my eyes, but you
have to believe it for yourself, my love."

Are You Exceptional?

Crystals have always been an important connection for us, both of us claiming the title Rock Hound. Our FNP is also a Metaphysician and has a strong working knowledge of the healing power of crystals. Many different stones and crystals are strewn throughout her office: on shelves, the top of desks, tables, and display cases.

At our business, we have stones scattered throughout the space, all placed strategically and with intent. We named our business Step Stone for a reason and we love that our services could be a step stone on the path to someone's self-discovery and healing expression. We also knew the power of having stones and crystals in the rooms, the amplification and facilitation of energy movement part of the unique energetic field we created.

One of the activities we both loved was hunting for crystals or stones. Whether it was digging for crystals at Crystal Park in Montana or finding beautiful agates along the beaches on the Oregon coast, we shared a common passion and love for the stones, crystals, and Earth. The real truth behind our passion was understanding the energetic properties of the stones. Being empathic, I feel the energy of crystals and stones. I know the power the Earth holds, ready and waiting to assist us. I design stone jewelry and became a Certified Crystal Practitioner and Crystal Reiki Master because of my connection to the remarkable energetic properties and conduit crystals and stones exemplify.

Jack frequently wore a stone necklace and bracelets I had designed for him because he understood the support they brought in all aspects of life: mental, emotional, physical, and spiritual. He loved the musician's necklace I created for him. He wore it often when he played music and swore he could feel more creative inspiration.

I viewed Jack as an exceptional soul but when I started reading from the book *Love, Medicine and Miracles* by Bernie Siegel, he stopped me. I was concerned as I felt this did not bode well for his strength of conviction toward healing. I sensed a form of defeat in his words and did not push the issue past my acknowledgment of his special, unique soul. I knew he had to come to terms within himself around who he was, who he came to be, and why he was here dealing with cancer now. Only he could determine the reasons and only he could create the miracle that would be his healing.

We are all exceptional souls. Living on Planet Earth at this time takes a form of courage and fortitude beyond most people's awareness.

September 10, 2019

My love, your loss of appetite is starting to be a big problem for you. I am now going to the store every day to pick up something else your stomach might tolerate as I watch your food selections going by the wayside, becoming narrowed by indigestion. You try a few bites of one of your favorites and then start coughing. I begin juicing, hoping to provide you with some nutrients. At least you can drink the juice right now.

Jozy comes by today, thrilled about his new Taylor Baby Grand guitar made of Koa Wood. It is amazing! He wants to show you so you can begin the journey of recovery and play the music the two of you both feel so drawn to create together. He purchased that guitar on the dream of music collaboration with you. You sparked his passion for playing again, and he was so looking forward to your mentorship. He had not even played the guitar with his own hands when he handed it to you. Although you are mostly bedridden with fatigue, you lovingly take the guitar and christen his new family member with a beautiful guitar lick, one I quietly capture on film. I am so grateful to have this short snippet of time to hold dear. I am not sure what the future will bring. We hold each other through the night, and I feel safe in your arms as though maybe this is all a bad dream.

Love as Energy

The human body has a remarkable capacity for resilience despite health challenges; the human spirit carries the capability to rise above drama, fear, the paradigm of death. What does death mean anyway? If all we are is this carbon-based form then yes, the form dies from this existence when it is done. But no, what I know beyond any doubt is that we are so much more than this physical form.

Science has proven we radiate an energy field beyond our physical form that can be measured by sensitive magnetometers. The body's magnetic field also known as the aura, can be seen by many people and photographed with appropriate equipment. The field surrounding us carries information just as a radio wave carries sound or a television signal carries information that is translated into pictures. That information is unseen yet is a tangible experience when filtered through a receiver like an antenna or a cable. We do not question the validity of those energy waves moving through the air, but many people often dismiss their own aura as something in the realm of woo woo, not to be believed or taken seriously.

The auric field is indeed real and has the capacity to share information as well as magnetize other energy frequencies toward us. Jack was able to draw toward him energies that helped him be strong despite his deteriorating body. We both held the insight we are not just human but are light beings, or souls, having a human experience in a physical body. That awareness was what helped him draw support from his family of light, those higher-level beings who are ready and waiting to answer a call for help. With that support, he was able to keep his spirits up, his quick wit intact.

We found laughter in moments that could have made us cry but Jack kept his sense of humor and would remark with sarcasm, "Well, another one bites the dust," referring to his loss of food options. We made a game of learning what foods his body would tolerate.

That afternoon, when Jozy stopped by with a new guitar, I relished the moment of seeing Jack play it for him. Jack had been his guitar instructor and they became fast friends, sharing a profound, loving connection as two souls who recognized each other. They discovered other lifetimes together with rich history. It all made sense as to why their current life expression was so powerfully connected, love of music a passionate thread bounding them together in this Now time.

Again, we are so much more than our physical form. We are souls who have moved into human form to experience this Now-time dimensional field, the third dimension as it is known. We all carry divinity within us. If we are breathing, we carry a spark of the divine, but we live in a free will Earth experiment. That means we choose how we live our lives, what we believe, and how we express. Our spirit guides, angels, the higher light-being families are always with us in support but they do not interfere with our choices. That divine connection is experienced through the body and our intuition, which can be activated and enhanced by our breath, breathing into the heart space, the center of our body's energy system. The key is to ask for connection and help. We must intend to connect with them through choice.

September 11, 2019

My love, you have been struggling with what we thought were hiccups for a few days now. The constant coughing and hiccups are wracking your body with spasms, and they seem to be more than just a hiccup now. The contractions appear tied to your breath, and we cannot get a handle on stopping them. It is becoming hard for you to talk without going into spasm, robbing precious breath from your lungs. Talking is one of our relationship's gifts, one of our best skills, so it is hard to see you struggle to speak. I know you have so much to say, so much to share, so many thoughts left hanging. Maybe if we try a new type of medication? You are still frequently coughing up blood, pneumonia and cancer making their presence known. You are growing weaker by the day, but I still hold the light of healing for you, giving you Reiki energy treatments many times a day and throughout the night. They seem to comfort you.

Communication

I was hyper-vigilant in watching Jack through this ever-increasing challenge of breathing. His hiccups were causing huge issues in his ability to talk. Talking is what we did best in our relationship so this was a monumental shift in how we communicated and a heartbreaking reality of his cancer-filled lungs. Staying positive was becoming much harder and

I found myself wavering despite how strong I wanted to be for his sake.

At times I would forget and ask him a question; of course, he would answer, or at least attempt to answer, but the spasms would take over, rendering him unable to form words, his body wrenching in pain. We started to work with basic sign language. I asked yes and no questions and he nodded or shook his head.

We became adept at looking into each other's eyes and sharing. Most of the time, I knew what he was trying to get across without speaking. I was in awe of how much we learned to communicate through only our eyes, telepathic lines opening even more than they already were between us.

The way we communicate is fascinating and I became aware of how much we use our speech, how easy it is to transfer information by structured sound, words, and language. What we were learning to do, though, was to understand each other through a different form of connection: that of the body, the facial expressions, the eyes. It is often said that the eyes are the window into the soul. In our world, that was a fact. I could look at Jack and understand an entire packet of information he was sending me telepathically. Many couples learn to do that after being together for a period of time, saying something before the other has a chance to verbalize the same thought. My dad used to joke around with my mom saying, "Geez, will you get out of my head!" I believe, as people become more intuitive, we will witness that type of communication happening even more.

We still talked because Jack wanted to share so much, his soul finding an internal resolve in an uncooperative body. He was frustrated with the spasms, the hiccups, the coughing up of blood. The medications the doctors had prescribed were not reducing the intensity of the chaos within his body.

A comfort to him was always the Reiki healing, a light touch, an understanding gaze, loving hands holding space for his wracked body. I also started diffusing essential oils, particularly the oils known to help with breathing and calming the nervous system. We kept the meditative music and nature scenes playing in the background on the TV unless we were watching a show. His care and support were my 24-hour task now.

September 12, 2019

Today has not started as planned. You made an appointment to take our Toyota 4-Runner to have the worn-out starter replaced. You want the vehicle to be ready for me to sell should you not make it. We had planned to go together, but we end up with a timing conflict with a building inspection; one of us needs to be present at home. You reassure me you are fine to drive to Missoula for the car appointment, so I let go and trust you will be okay. We stay in touch, and I plan to meet you after the inspection so we can go to your Medical Intuitive appointment. Wires cross, and the inspector did not arrive when he said he would. I become angry. I seldom get mad with life, but I do today—my anger toward outside circumstances out of my control. I am wracked with concern for you, your safety.

I call you, and you tell me you are standing in the sunshine, your face feeling the warmth, while they finish with the car service. You are okay, well enough to drive the one-hour trip home. I pull myself together and call the inspector. I tell him I will get him to come to inspect the building after your doctor's appointment. My biggest concern is you, my love. I am frustrated with what has happened. When I see you, though, I let it all go. I am just so grateful you are okay, and we can go to your next appointment together.

The Medical Intuitive appointment goes very well. I record the session so we can listen to it later and follow what she recommends, follow through with what resonates with your soul.

Tonight, the hiccups begin again. They are incessant; nothing you do helps. We research numerous home remedies and try them all. You experience only moments of reprieve, and then there is the constant coughing. Your comfort is growing more and more distant and yet you maintain a positive attitude. I am amazed at your strength.

Finding Flow Can Be Challenging

Resilience: the ability to recover quickly from difficulty, spring back or be flexible while remaining strong. This day put my professional resiliency training to the test. Even more than the day of the cancer diagnosis, I found my raw, jagged emotions rising. I seldom experience anger as I am adept at stepping back and seeing the bigger picture, understanding that life throws curve balls. It is a matter of dodging the impact through breath to maintain stability. But this day, staying centered was not an easy task for me.

I found myself angry at the turn of events and had to keep reminding myself that all the moving parts were just not synchronized the way I wanted them to be. Jack was the calm one, reminding me he was fine. He was able to drive and, once there, he could stand outside in the sunshine, feeling the warmth on his face, absorbing all he could from the beauty of nature. I softened and my concern for him subsided.

However, I did voice my frustration and stood my ground on meeting the building inspector, requesting a time change based on our needs, not his. I had already stayed behind to meet him without success due to his priorities. I felt it was important for both of us to keep Jack's appointments with our FPN and a Medical Intuitive (MI). I made sure we could meet the inspector afterward. He was accommodating and showed compassion for our situation; my frustration melted away in recognizing it was okay for me to feel what I had felt. My whole life was teetering on the edge of huge loss.

The Medical Intuitive was in California, so we were online for the session. This woman has the gift of seeing a person's medical issues and understanding the root emotional basis for physical conditions. Jack and I felt this was an essential step in his ability to transform what his body was experiencing. If he could identify his illness's emotional root cause, he believed he stood a chance to shift it. Jack and I knew if he could get to the core issue underneath his cancer then he, his soul, would have choice in healing. It has been shown that around 80% of all disease has origins in stress, a root emotional stressor that has not been recognized or resolved in some fashion. We were looking forward to what this session would reveal.

His discomfort was high and breathing labored but he maintained his composure. He found it harder to focus as his attention was being diverted much of the time to dealing with his body, trying to maintain homeostasis. Because he had almost drowned when he was young, Jack's biggest fear was the possibility of suffocation from his increasing lung restriction. He was also losing the desire to eat, had some concerns about a popping sensation in his heart area, and was starting to feel overwhelmed by the pain. It was growing more and more challenging to pull out of the physicality of his body. He described feeling as though he was in a runaway train. Jack had numerous questions for the MI. The body symptoms seemed to have a mind of their own and he was curious if these physical signs were his signal. Was he staying or leaving? Was this his exit point? Would he have awareness if it was time? Could he leave his body while remaining conscious during the process of his passage?

The MI was quick to get into the thick of his cancer challenges. I asked if I could record the session along with taking copious notes. I did not want to miss any crucial details. I was glad to have that recording as Jack and I both listened again to be clear about what she said. Our minds were having to track so many details now.

At first, Jack thought much of the emotional tumult was related to his rocky relationship with his mother. He insisted the MI look at that facet of his childhood but she kept coming back to his father. Her guides told her his key issue happened during an incident with his father when he was nine years old. Jack tried to argue with her but she insisted he had done the healing work related to his mother and all was good. She was sure the event with his unattached and distant father had emotional ties to the cancer in his lungs. The more she discussed this with him, the more an internal lightbulb illuminated his eyes. His father had hurt Jack so severely it took his breath away, literally creating an emotional pattern in his life of not ever being able to breathe into who he was, who he wanted to be. He could never breathe into his essence because it felt unsafe.

The MI stated no judgment was attached to or against anyone involved but Jack had no foundational security in his world. What happened at nine catapulted him into popping in and out of his body, this third-dimensional reality, into other realms. His ability to experience being multidimensional was the very gift that brought his spiritual awakening. He had thought this ability was normal for everyone. The fact he felt he had to run, go somewhere else while trapped in his form, catalyzed his connection to Spirit, which then became a lifelong empathic awareness and search for answers. She said he carried the energy of a wizard; he also had a very masculine entity or guide who had been with him since age nine. Jack had been aware of this guide many times in his life.

The child aspect of Jack was running around outside of his body; it was important he calm and support this younger version of himself. It was the child who wanted to leave the body and this life, not the adult aspect in the Now. If Jack was to have a fighting chance at survival, the child needed to breathe and feel safe inside the body.

The MI then began to discuss ways for Jack to work with his inner child to heal the abandonment issues he had felt. There was a feeling of deep sorrow in Jack about his dad never accepting him and it was important he connect with that vibrational energy to heal the lifelong wound. The child needed acknowledgment from a male energy; not feeling worthy to receive masculine love and support created an imbalance in his system.

The healing activity we were to do together was for me to hold Jack, creating a feeling of security while we both focused on the vision of Jack at nine years old. Jack was to imagine his child self receiving these words by someone as a proxy of his father: "I see you; I acknowledge you; I love you." Jack was to reply: "I accept that."

This activity was to be repeated until Jack was in a space of acceptance and non-judgment. When he was ready, he said: "Dad, I love you. Thank you for the lessons. I'm giving your stories back to you." Proxy for dad would then say: "I love you. Thank you for the lessons. I take back my story and I'm giving you back your power." Jack would then say: "I love you. Thank you. I am taking my power back. I own my power." He was to visualize swallowing that power in the form of a beautiful crystal.

41

The MI suggested a second activity of calling in his warrior of light to soothe and assist the child inside Jack. We were to light a beeswax candle and, with his third eye chakra and his heart chakra, he could chant the words: "The warrior and I are one. I and the warrior are one." Jack could use this mantra whenever he felt up to it.

Nature was also a strong bond for Jack; he resonated with the unique wizard-like energy of trees. We were to go out in nature if at all possible. If that was too difficult, he was to gaze at a picture of a tree. Viewing the photo would help him connect back to the wizard energy he was so accustomed to feeling while in the woods. The suggested mantra was: "I and the tree are one. The tree and I are one." This would help him unleash the magic inside. We knew just the picture to use; it was one Jack took during one of our trips to the Oregon Coast and into the Redwood forest in northern California. It was of me standing in front of a huge, majestic, Redwood tree, one of his favorite photos.

If Jack could swallow these empowerments, he could decide whether to stay or leave; it would be his choice in full awareness instead of helplessness. At that point, Jack would find whether his purpose was to stay or to go from a balanced perspective.

She suggested Jack and I do an open-heart chakra ceremony together in support of our journey as beloveds. Facing each other, we would place a hand on each other's hearts, sending divine love to each other. Using the power of stones, we were to place a piece of selenite on Jack's heart chakra with a small chunk of moldavite on top. We would send healing energy and love into his heart chakra, soothing all aspects needing the high vibration of love to transmute and empower his body, mind, and soul.

We thanked our FNP and the MI for all of this insight. The session ended with lots of gratitude being shared and, while we were at the checkout paying for the service, Jack purchased a beautiful large green Malachite stone. When I asked him what it was for, he handed it to me and said, "This might be the last gift I am able to give you." He wanted so much to honor our love and intuitively knew this stone held properties that would assist me.

We headed back to our place to meet the inspector, our minds reeling with all this new information to digest, and with new pain and cough syrup prescriptions. After the inspection, I looked up the properties of Malachite on www.ablecrystals.com. It is a "stone of transformation," assisting the bearer in changing situations and providing for the transfer of sacred information leading to spiritual evolution. It stimulates instinctive and intuitive reasoning, allowing for change which facilitates advancement. It also represents fidelity in love and friendship. Malachite is an excellent balancer on all levels. Jack just knew.

That evening the trigger for hiccup spasms was ever-present and could be set off by any number of activities: eating, talking, breathing.

September 13, 2019

Based on the information we received from the Medical Intuitive, I shop to get the items we decide to use in the emotional and energetic work we are doing. I gather some essential stones that carry a lot of meaning for you. I find beeswax candles to do some of the emotional trauma releasing activities and items to perform some of the suggested detoxes.

Your best friend, Jozy, comes by to see you. He is doing his darndest to help keep you strong and fighting. We perform one of the activities we know you need to do in addressing the root cause of the cancer: the emotional trauma from a father who was never there for you emotionally. When you were nine, an incident with your father became part of a lifelong pattern of holding your breath, being unable to breathe into who you are here to be, the very foundation of your life not being seen or supported.

Jozy takes the role of your father as the two of you act out a new scenario. As your father, he looks you square in the eyes and says, "I see you, I acknowledge you, I love you, please forgive me, it was not your fault, I take back what was mine!" Then, my love, you say to your father, "I acknowledge you, I see you, I forgive you, and I take back my life." As I sit in witness to what is happening before my eyes, I am struck with the depths of healing taking place at that moment: healing a lifetime of feeling you could not breathe into who you were, a lifetime of never feeling good enough, a lifetime in search of your sovereign being, a quest that ultimately led you to find your spiritual journey. I see that pain melt away in your eyes. I know the love exchange between you and your father, who is portrayed by your friend. There are no words.

When Jozy leaves, he still believes you will fight this and not give up. He carries a warrior's energy and knows you have that in you too. But then, my love, we talk after he leaves.

You gaze into my eyes with an intensity I feel course through my body; I can sense what is coming. My heart racing; I don't want to hear it. Please, I don't want to listen to what I know is inevitable. You lovingly say to me, "You know, my love, this is not about my survival; it is about my passing. Leaving this planet is my path. Death is what we both came here to do. You know this. This passage, too, is part of our journey together, my transition out of this form. You know this is part of your journey going forward, the work you are here to do in the world. You know this, don't you? You are aware there is no other way for you to gain the wisdom, courage, and compassion you will carry in helping others, right?"

I nod my head, yes. I cannot speak, tears flowing down my cheeks, my throat choked with quiet sobs. And yet, at the deepest part of my being, I know. I do know this to be true; we intended death to be a part of our journey, part of the reason we came together, to experience this side of the power of unconditional, divine love.

You say to me, "My love, I don't want to leave you, but this is happening, and I am asking you to help me pass. I want to do this in the most peaceful, conscious, and spiritual way possible. I do not want it to drag on; my body is weak, and I need your help. Will you do this with me?"

I look at you in complete surrender to what is taking place. With all the love, gratitude, and courage I am capable of feeling, I say, "Of course I will be here with you every step of the way, every precious moment, every second. I will not leave your side! I am your wingman, remember?" I smile at you through eyes glazed with tears.

The rest of the night, we hold each other. Every time your emotions arise, the breathing spasms start, so we remain calm and in a state of undying love while we hold each other close. We wonder if we will be able to stay connected after your death. Will we continue our relationship from a whole different reality, knowing our soul connection is more than just this life expression, bridging dimensions?

Acceptance Through Love

What took place this day forever changed me. I had no idea how much courage I had within until I witnessed it. I had no idea of the depths to which love can go until I experienced it. I had no idea of the vastness of the human heart until I lived it.

Jack performed incredible feats of emotional healing on this day, tapping into the spiritual warrior side of his essence in a way I had never observed before. It was as if the wizard, Jack, was wielding his magical staff and the power that spewed forth in his actions changed the world, rippled out into the cosmos. I marveled at watching him with his friend, seeing the unfathomable depths to which both men dove, the powerful spiritual beings I loved and adored. I was honored to witness Jack in his moments of awakening into a sage's wisdom and in seeing the vulnerability and acceptance of his inner child. He became the solid rock amidst the turbulent storm that was our life. I was desperately holding on, the beacon of light and love he needed to remain solid.

Jozy was ready to take up the sword of health; he knew Jack had the power to move through the cancer. What Jozy and I had not realized was that Jack's accomplishment of the healing activities suggested by the MI would yield a decision that would shake us to the core.

And yet, the main player in the show made his decision. Jack became aware of his soul's purpose, the journey he chose, and he was leaving his body.

News of the cancer was a shock to both of us, but it was nothing compared to the unwavering and loving request he made of me this day. Death was to be our experience, his conscious awareness of a soul path that included my soul path as well.

How could I welcome his passing with the open arms of surrender? How would I be able to move forward in my life without him?

When I looked into his eyes, into his soul, the divine light of awareness infiltrated my being to the core of my essence and I remembered. I remembered our soul contract, the amount of love it would take to traverse this path, and that we chose it. We chose to step into this aspect of divine love that exists beyond time and space. I could not deny the knowledge of that remembering, no matter how gut-wrenching the days ahead.

I knew the expansion of love then, a love not bound by form but of the divine, universal heart, the compassionate heart that knows how to say goodbye when goodbye is in the highest service to that divine love.

I found my warrior goddess on that day, the one who stands on the front line of change with the armor of courage, torch in hand, lighting the way for others. This day, I began holding the torch for my love, whose death was now a given, and his tasks of letting go of the physical body an unknown card to be played. By choice, I would be his death-passage guide.

September 14, 2019

We spend the day just working at keeping you comfortable. I am setting the stage for you. We had already placed a temporary bed in your music studio, allowing you to be in the space you love so much. We are completing the necessary tasks. Your life force is growing weaker with each passing moment, and yet I sense a feeling of peace in you. You are doing the internal mental and emotional work to let your body release.

At one point during the day, you sit up in the bed because you cannot lie down due to the spasms and coughing. I decide to sit next to you, and we make a pact, a promise that carries wisdom beyond time and space. We will do the death process like we do life together, with open hearts, courage, and an awareness of the bigger picture, the spiritual nature of who we are. I vow, with every fiber of my soul, to help you.

You work with the black Kyanite stone gifted by a dear friend. You are holding it on your solar plexus, the area between your heart and your stomach. I am watching you. Your eyes are closed as you are in meditation. I am in complete surrender to the moment and in awe of your resolve. Something inside compels me to move to your side. I place my hands on top of yours. From someplace within, a place in me that carries the strength of the goddess, I start to channel words that flow directly out of my heart. "It is okay that you are leaving this planet. I understand our soul contract. You can do this, my love. You are a spiritual warrior who can create magic. You have created magic throughout our time together. You know how to accomplish this transition process, so tap into that part of your being and remember. Your body knows how to let go, so work toward that goal. It is all okay. I am going to be fine. It is our journey. I honor you and will always love you. It is okay for you to leave, my love. I release you to your highest expression, the soul that is ready to release this dense body."

In the crisp evening air, we walk outside to see the Harvest Moon. I move behind you with my arms encircled around your belly, love you, hold you. I bury my face in the soft skin in the back of your neck, breathing in the scent of you. One of my favorite things is to hug you from behind and press my face against that tender spot on your neck. I think back to other the times we stood outside, looking at the moon, clouds, or birds while in this position. I take in the feel of your body against mine, I tune my senses into the energy exchange we share, understanding that moments like this are for me to treasure as long as I am able, as long as you are here.

We are experiencing the journey of conscious death, my love.

Finding the Depths of Spirit

As I mentioned earlier, we knew stones carry powerful energetic properties, but we did not necessarily understand all of the nuances each particular stone holds. All we knew was that certain stones carried a powerful energy exchange for Jack. Near his bed, he had me place crystals he had found, the smokey quartz, the recorder quartz, the amethyst I had gifted him, the azurite I found for him while in New Mexico. He had me place his necklaces by the photo of me in the Redwoods. He wore the ring I had made for him from the beautiful blue agate he found on the Oregon Coast. All of these stones meant something to him, so they were constantly near. We had added the selenite and moldavite to the side table as well. The Reiki Peace Grid was stationed nearby.

One stone we had never worked with was Black Kyanite. That stone was gifted to Jack by our FNP, the one who is a Metaphysician. She handed him the stone as we left her office the day we had the Medical Intuitive session. She looked at Jack with teary eyes, and when he offered to pay for the stone, she said no, it was her gift. She turned to walk away as her emotions began welling up inside. Jack was a special person and his kindness touched those who encountered him. He complimented her and told her what a unique soul she was, how much his work with her had meant to him; he was blessed to know her.

That day we made a promise. I was ready to support him in whatever way possible with all the tools at my disposal, so when he asked me to come and sit at the edge of the bed next to him, I did not hesitate. We held hands and gazed into each other's eyes as the promise was made: we would do death like we did life, together, as one. We had no idea what the death process would look like, what his body would go through, but we were hopeful he would remember how to let go. While both of us had lost loved ones, we had not been active in the actual death process; this was a whole new learning experience. I was silently praying to the divine and the higher aspect of him: please make this journey as fast as possible for his sake. While I was praying for his release, I knew I was losing the man I saw as my soul mate, my other half, two ends of the same soul spectrum.

The Black Kyanite meant something beyond our awareness; we did not have time to look it up before I found Jack using it on his solar plexus chakra in a deep meditative state. It did not matter at that moment. What mattered was the powerful energy I felt emanating from his body while a surge moved through me. I was guided to sit next to him and place my hand on his. The words I spoke carried a strength beyond anything I had felt before and I had a knowing of our eternal journey, a commitment to a greater purpose. Jack and I played out our roles to create a display of divine love for others to see. Jack knew I would be writing about this death walk he was taking and I was assisting. The bigger picture was ever-present in our minds. In those moments of stepping back from the Becki in physical form to the soul Becki, my suffering and grief were dampened.

When we finished our shamanistic soul empowerment, I looked up the energetic properties of Black Kyanite. I was in awe of the synchronicity of life and the gift of enlightened spiritual tools.

> In Judy Hall's book *The Crystal Bible 2*, she describes Black Kyanite as "an Earth tool to assist in moving into the between-life state, to access and manifest the current soul plan and release soul imperatives that no longer serve a purpose. This stone shows the karma currently being created by present choices and assists in foreseeing the outcome of a soul plan."

How perfect the gift for his remembering his soul plan and how to leave the physical realm!

The light of the harvest moon amplified our daytime activities and we shared in the magic the crisp night air seemed to signal. The bright shining orb in the night sky encircled by a rainbow colored halo felt sacred, an acknowledgment of souls remembering their divine journey.

September 15, 2019

You ask Jozy to join us for dinner, telling him we need to talk. When he arrives, you start telling him about the journey you now take. I sit in my chair, ready to support both of you with the intense discussion. You say to him that, as a spiritual warrior, you know this is about your passing. He sits in silence, taking it all in. Tears well in his eyes. I know that, deep in his heart, he had been holding out for the miracles card to be played. This news is a whole different gig.

My love, you are so kind and compassionate with him as you share your request, "I am asking you to help me. Being a part of my death is not anything required. Believe me, I do not ask lightly. I know the depths of what I am asking of you, my dear friend. It is okay for you to get up right now and walk away; tell me you cannot do this; you do not want to be a part of this. It is totally okay with me if you do. I love you dearly and would not think less of you in any way, but the reality is I am going to die, and I need support. I do not need the energy of you holding on, making it harder for me to let go. So, do you want to join Becki and me on this last journey we take here together, or do you need to go, walk away from conscious death? Remember, I love you dearly, no matter what."

I move over near Jozy so I can comfort him, hold him for a moment. He has never lost anyone close to him, never faced death before. We all sit in silence for what seems like a no-time reality, our bodies all breathing laboriously.

He just sits there, taking in your words. Finally, he says, "I am in! I'm not going anywhere. We are the three amigos. I will do what you need me to do. I will help however I can. I am not leaving."

I look at you, my love, and see colossal relief wash over you. The two people you love most in the world are in this room with you, standing with you as you say goodbye to life, neither of us leaving your side during your time of greatest need.

A dear friend Susan, who had lost her husband some time ago, gave us a copy of the Tibetan Book of Living and Dying. Jozy, Jack, and I sit together and I read passages from the book. We all must approach this from a higher perspective, from a place of Spirit. Conscious death is what you want, my love, and your warrior spirit is asking both your friend and me to step into that type of energy. This process will be intense, demanding, something none of us has experienced, the release of a body in death. And yet we are all in, knowing we are doing something unique, something special, something few people witness in this way: the way of honoring the spirit in passage back home.

We all sit down to dinner, and you eat a few bites but start going into breathing spasms. Little do we know this is the last time you eat food, your body beginning to make its way to shutting down.

You have so much you want to share with us after dinner, but the spasms start every time you talk, and you struggle to get words out. Finally, I say, "Don't talk right now, just rest. We know you. We love you. Just relax and rest." Our eyes all meet, and the unspoken energy exchange is intense, recognizing the immensity of the moments ahead, every cell in my body vibrating with an unknown conscious awareness.

I walk our friend to the door, and we hug each other, our bodies holding on while shaking with emotion, knowing that what we have accepted will forever change us. We both hope we have the strength needed to walk this last journey with you, my love.

Taking Action

Our death passage contract was known only to the two of us, the promise made yesterday between two beloveds on a profoundly intimate final passage. But we knew there was a third, another soul who needed to have the option to participate: Jozy, the other point in the energetic triangle.

How do you share with someone that death is your choice? As humans, we are so conditioned to fight until the bitter end, to never give up, to stay in the game, especially when it comes to life. Other cultures and different timelines have honored the death process, celebrating the transition from the density of form into the high vibrational light of who we truly are, souls having a human moment here on earth.

The flip side is that many people struggle to let their loved ones go. It is heartbreaking to lose a loved one. I believe it is easier to be the one leaving because, once over the threshold, those souls are back home. We are the ones left on the odyssey of life without them. I would never tell you it is easy to let go. I wondered at my ability to move in that direction, and yet I had a strong enough energetic connection to Jack that I knew it would be all the more challenging for him to say goodbye to life if I did not let go. Being empathic, we had such a strong connection; no words were needed to understand the others' feelings. He would be able to feel my pull toward him, holding him, wanting him to stay, and he understood he needed clear skies for this flight plan. He asked that of me. So, my goal was to keep letting go of his physical presence, the idea of a future with him, the plans we had made together, dreams we had envisioned. The task was gargantuan.

When we called on Jozy to come over for dinner and conversation, I knew shock would wash over him, battering his steadfast resolve for assistive healing. He was still ready to fight the good fight with Jack. Jack's decision to embrace his death passage could feel like a defeat to him, a giving up. But in reality, this was a genuine acceptance of Jack's soul path and a warrior's death was the plan. Stepping gracefully into conscious death passage was to be the good fight ahead.

I was focused on Jack but, as he shared the decision with Jozy, my attention turned. I moved close to hold Jozy through the inevitable tears. Death had not even been an option in his mind, so the impact on his entire body and energetic system was massive.

Jack knew this could send Jozy in a broken escape from the reality staring him in the face and breathing heavily down his neck. He was prepared for that possibility, holding love and acceptance for his friend's choice. Jack knew what he was asking of both of us, the magnitude of courage we would all need to accomplish this final passage. We sat in silence; the only sound was the labored breathing from Jack's body.

Then Jozy sat straight up and said he was not leaving. That he was in, that this was our destined path together as a team, the three amigos bonded in loving friendship. We all felt relief and allowed several minutes for reality to integrate.

Susan, who kindly gifted us with *The Tibetan Book of Living and Dying* by Sogyal Rinpoche, was comforted by this book. I read aloud some passages I thought might help guide the three of us as we dove into dark and unknown waters.

Dinner took on the finality of our last meal together.

September 16, 2019

The sun is shining today. You are standing and walking with my help. You are keen on getting the Toyota 4-Runner, affectionately called Stui, cleaned out while showing me what I need to know to sell it. You ask me to make selling your vehicle a priority after you pass as I will not need it, and the money will come in handy with me not working right now. No one is out back, so you feel safe to venture out; you do not want to see anyone. As we share memories of our adventures in Stui, I start feeling melancholy, heartbroken, tears welling. I blurt out, "I really wish we could make one more trip to the Oregon Coast, to the place we love so much, the place where we both feel connected, where our love blossomed and expressed itself. Maybe if I drive, we could just go now." I am feeling desperate, praying for more experiences with you.

You gaze into my eyes with love but beseechingly say, "Please, my love, don't make leaving this life any harder than it already is. I won't make it to the coast. My body is too far down the path. I am having a hard enough time letting go of you and this amazing world, nature and all the beauty. Please don't bring up the things I love doing in this life. I need to let life here go."

"Oh, my love, I am so sorry. I can't even imagine what you must be going through, letting go of your very life force. I will honor your request and not bring those things up. As hard as it is for me to lose you, you are saying goodbye to all the things in life you treasure, goodbye to life as we know it." Silently I reassure myself I can do this for you. I can be strong and walk these last steps with you, right by your side, all the while understanding a part of me is dying with you, my life forever changed.

Again, I move into my favorite position, behind you with my arms encircled around your belly, love you, hold you. My face immediately moves into the soft skin in the back of your neck, and I breathe in your essence. My body is taking in the memory of this moment, the feel of our bodies embracing as we watch clouds float by in the brilliant blue sky. You remark how beautiful this world is and how you are going to miss moments like this. How much longer will we have, my love?

In the afternoon, you are sitting at the edge of the bed. You motion me to get the guitar you named Angel that is hanging on the wall. You want to play for me, the song that moves me to tears every time I hear it. From the moment that song was birthed from your hands, it resonated with my soul. You wrote it for me. I could sit and listen to you play for hours; the feelings created through your gift of music are magical. I am always transfixed, taken away to a

61

place beyond this dimension by the sheer power of your music.

You rest the guitar in your arms, holding it lovingly, saying hello to this member of your family. All of your guitars are like family members to you, each with its unique personality and life force signature. I hand you Angel.

I sit down next to you. You try valiantly to play the song, but your fingers are having a difficult time moving. The strength is fading from your hands, those hands that carry magical energy. How often have I held them, kissed them, and marveled at them, those hands that bring me so much pleasure, the energy emanating powerful life force?

As hard as you try, you cannot play. You look at me and hand me Angel. With tear-filled eyes, you say, "Put it away! Just put it away!" I take the guitar from your hands and begin shaking as I hang it on its stand, feeling your heart breaking as you say goodbye to the ability to play music. It has kept you on the planet during the most difficult times, as you used your music to transform the trauma, the darkness. It is all I can do to not wholly break down in front of you as I know what this means. The reality that you are done with this life comes crashing down around both of us.

Letting Go

The day started with a phone call to our FNP to inform her about the constant hiccups that are ever-present now. We had tried every home remedy we could find and nothing was working for Jack. He was exhausted but carried the resolve of a man on the most important mission of his life, how to die with grace.

I informed our FNP that Jack's decision was one of death, transition was now his goal. She told me she already knew he was leaving. She had received a call from the MI two days after our session informing her Jack was dying. During his session, she had seen the color green in his auric field, a sign that healing energy was still in place; healing was still an option for him. But, two days later his auric field was gray, a sign the energetic body was starting the death process. He still carried the light of his soul but the body was letting go and shutting down his energy centers, his chakras. He had made his decision with clear intent and his body was responding. Healing his emotional trauma was his signal for choice and he had the green light to leave, free of that emotional burden.

Today was a day of letting go. Jack was guiding me through the release of his vehicle, showing me what I needed to know to sell it. Stui, named after one of Jack's favorite mentors, Stuart Wilde, was a part of our memorable adventures, the vehicle we took crystal hunting and driving the backroads of

Montana. Jack loved this car and had spent many hours devoted to its care and upkeep. I was grateful he had been able to take one last drive a few days ago.

He relished being outside and breathing what air he could pull into his lungs. I watched in anguish. The more we chatted about the car, the deeper my melancholy became; a massive wave of desperation enveloped me, my body feeling sick with loss. I took several deep breaths trying to maintain my composure, recognizing that breath was easy for me while I was watching my love struggle to breathe. It was a surreal moment, time becoming slow; the things I thought were important in life just vanished as my heartbreak raised its head.

I desperately wanted to just take Jack away, sweep him up in my arms and drive like hell to the coast one last time. The Oregon Coast had meant so much to us. I felt bowled over with not wanting my life with him to end like this, so fast, so soon. I blurted out my desire to him, thinking maybe there was one last chance for adventure.

His compassion for me was shining through his eyes as he gently reminded me of his reality. He was letting go of life itself and he knew his time was near. I had to keep letting go of him, of our life together. Death was the adventure we were undertaking. Despite having moments of feeling how unfair the whole cancer reality was, I was brought back to face my love with an awareness of his truth, our truth. I continued to step into his shoes, knowing I would have my time to let down my shield, rest into my pain once he was gone. For now, my greatest gift to him was to continue to release my own needs through an open and pure divine love. My task was to step back and become the observer to the bigger picture we chose to come together to experience. Jack knew and somewhere deep in my soul I also had that remembering. I found grace and courage in an instant through his beseeching gaze into my eyes.

I burned into my memory those significant intimate connections: the feel of his soft neck, the smell of his skin, the warmth of his body. The small moments became treasured and each minute we held each other, I vowed never to forget.

As the sun was shining, we held each other in recognition of the extraordinary journey we had together. We thought of the magic we carried and of the soul connection we experienced. I never wanted that moment to end. And then Jack tired; he needed to go back inside to rest.

It felt as though all we did this day was let go of life. So many aspects of our multi-faceted human existence were on the chopping block, waiting to be the next to disappear.

How can I even begin to explain the passion Jack felt for music, the part of his expression that held him here, on the planet. Many years ago, a dear mentor of mine, who is an empath and channel, had said, "If Jack loses his music, he loses his life. It is such an integral aspect of who he is. Music has kept him on the planet" Those words haunted me as the next aspect to his life was saying goodbye.

When he asked me to bring him his guitar, Angel, I was more than happy to oblige. I had spent many hours fully absorbed by the melodic playing of his soul. He had written several songs for me over the years but one, in particular, brought me to tears every time I listened to it and he knew I wanted to hear him play that part of him again. That melody was the one song he had not recorded in some fashion, always saying he would get to it when we finished building the studio. Now, the only way for me to hear it was directly from him or in my memory.

One of the most excruciating heartbreaks was to watch him try to play the song for me, his hands fumbling, his fingers not moving according to his innate instruction. For the first time, I saw defeat in those beautiful blue eyes as he handed Angel back to me, his attempt to send his love through sound vanquished. No words needed to be exchanged for me to understand what this meant for both of us.

Memory would be all I have. Letting go would be our shared sorrow.

September 17, 2019

We contacted your FNP yesterday to get a different medication for the spasms and now the prescription is ready. Nothing seems to be working to dissipate them so far, the cancer making breathing torturous.

I suddenly hear music while in the kitchen making coffee. I am immediately aware you have the guitar in hand and are playing my song, the one you tried to play yesterday. I stand there in silence because I do not want to disturb you from your moment, the one last time you hold Angel and play for me, pouring out your love to me through song. As I close my eyes and listen, my heart fills with gratitude that you had one more chance to be with the essence of your expression, hold that Angel in your arms, and express your feelings that are so powerful there are no words. I relish those few moments, for I know this is the last time you will play for me. It is a strange awareness to feel complete heartbreak and deep, abiding gratitude at the same moment. You stop playing, and as I walk into the room, I see you placing Angel on her hanger, a look of peace on your face. I smile and thank you. We do not speak about what just took place, both of us knowing another door closed. Spirit gifted you with one last beautiful experience of living and playing your soul song.

We make a quick trip to your doctor this morning for an injection intended to help with the spasms. It does not seem to decrease them much. What happens instead is that your personality changes from a loving and gentle demeanor to irritation and upset, the slightest little event causing you considerable emotional stress and anger. I have to keep reminding you what you are experiencing is related to the medication.

You decide not to use that medication again because a part of you knows how hard you had been on me in those moments. You mention to a friend you are not a nice person with that medication and do not want to hurt me; the last thing you want is to hurt me.

I was not aware you recorded a short video for me on September 6. I did not see it until today when you asked me to send a friend a text message. In your video message, you are aware this could go either way and you say how much you love me and how sorry you are that I am going down the cancer journey with you, knowing full well it includes hardships we would only find through experience. You tell me that, regardless of the outcome, you will see me soon on the other side. I watch through tears of anguish as I recognize your concern for me in this process, saying words that are not easy, so you record them for me to watch. You must have had an awareness this might be our goodbye even before we made our pact together. I love you so much for your concern for me. How is it that your love for me is your first concern even in your time of most significant challenge and physical pain? You are my warrior, my watchdog, my soul connection, my love! I treasure our love and can't even imagine my life without you, even though physical separation is the journey we take.

Gratitude

There have been many times in my life when I knew a higher power, spirit, angel, or other being was assisting me, providing solace and comfort along the way when I was weary or weak and beaten. This day was no exception.

When I heard Jack's music from the kitchen, I was taken into the realm of spiritual bliss while feeling my anguish at the same time. Jack was playing. The fact he was able to stand, walk, and retrieve his guitar unassisted was surprising, but the perfect execution of the song was divine. We both had help from our guides, those beings who had been around throughout our lives and who were supporting us now as we traveled the death walk together.

I was full of gratitude for Jack. His lifelong love of expressing sound was gifted one more time, but the real key to this surprise gift was his offering to me. He could have played any song but he chose the one I loved, the song he had played so many times while watching my tears flow, my heart open to receive his offering. He played the song he had attempted the day before when I sat next to him. This time he seized the moment and I listened from afar. The feeling I had was indescribable as I stood in silence, absorbing his love played out through his guitar Angel. Gratitude and anguish became my bedfellows.

The trip to our FNP was frantic. Jack's discomfort was extreme, hiccups and spasms challenging his air intake. I wasn't sure how he would make the trip, but he had the ability to manage high levels of pain; he carried a warrior's spirit. There were two critical tasks we needed to complete. One was to transfer the necessary documents from our FNP to get Hospice started and in place before Jack passed; the second was to try a new medication to ease his spasms.

The leg injection was a desperate measure intending to calm or at least reduce the severity of the physical response. Unfortunately, the medication had little impact on the target spasms but had a significant effect on Jack's personality. My kind, compassionate man became irritable, upset, and easily angered, my slightest misstep causing words of frustration to spew from his mouth. Wow! The man now sitting in the passenger seat was not the same man I drove to the appointment.

At this point, I used all my skills as a life coach to gently remind him this was a temporary feeling, his emotional upset related to the medication and not the situation. However, I was quietly aware this was probably a good release of tension for him. I allowed my awareness to guide my responses as the observer and not the Becki in physical form who might react or be triggered by his emotional upset. I was able to be patient, kind, and understanding while I prayed the medication side effects would wear off quickly.

Once we arrived home, I was able to help him back into bed rest. The repercussions on his attitude did eventually wear off and he was mindful of his behavior. He regretted his lack of kindness toward me; the last thing he wanted was to make this any harder on me than it already was. Another medication checked off the list.

In Jack's video message, he said what he was feeling from his heart and I experienced deep gratitude for his love and concern for me on this path we were to take. How fortunate to have that moment frozen in time, for me to watch when I feel the pull, to step into the sweet sorrow we shared.

Gratitude is a powerful, healing emotion experienced through the heart of our being, the connection to our soul. We are all so much stronger than we realize; in the face of adversity we find courage, resolve; we find HEART. When we find our heart and really step into the higher-level energies of love and compassion, we often find gratitude there, a gentle and silent antidote to our pain. Gratitude has a way of alchemizing and shifting awareness from our individual suffering to seeing life from a bigger perspective, one connected to Source, the divinity within connected to all.

This rollercoaster day had a full range of emotions. We experienced it all through awareness of our divine contract, our soul connection, our love, because we knew our time together was drawing short. How many days left now? When you are counting the precious minutes overshadowed by death, you put life into perspective and the small, petty nuisances and upsets are recognized for what they are; small, petty and temporary.

September 18, 2019

Our ER visit was two weeks ago, not two months. Now I sit here with a computer in my lap watching you breathe because just moments ago, you were not breathing. The spasm that has been gripping your diaphragm took hold for several seconds as you gasped for air. We both thought it might be the end. I am watching you, loving you, sending you healing energy while I pray for you to live one more day.

The Hospice representative is so kind. We are hustling to get documents in place to authorize only comfort measures with no resuscitation, no life-prolonging treatments, as you make the big journey home. My vigil, which began two weeks ago, has taken on a whole new level of required attunement. I type a few words and look across the bed at you. I hear you breathing heavily but not in spasm. You are resting. Your handsome face is yellowed and sunken from this excruciating journey, the lack of food, the coughing up of blood, telltale signs of a battle fought.

Despite seeing your physically shaken body in the death process, I find you as handsome as ever. I adore you! You are such a gift in my life. Even now, as I type, cry, type some more, I am deeply grateful I had 12 great years with you on this quest of discovery you and I came here to experience. My life was forever changed when our eyes met and we recognized each other, not from this realm but from beyond this physical plane of existence. We just knew our meeting

73

and joining in life was destined. The gift of who we came here to be as a unified couple, experiencing spiritual self-discovery while exploring the higher realms of life, is a journey few couples get to take together. We held a unique awareness, a knowing we came together for as long as it was meant to be. When it stopped working for either of us, it was okay to move on. People often said how fortunate we were to be traveling the self-discovery path together, to have a depth of connection beyond time. We have experienced life in the no-time, and I love that we could talk an entire day away and be amazed to discover it was evening. Where did our day go? Our day was truly living in the moment, a gift you taught me and one I find myself immersed in now as I watch you. I am painfully aware life has stopped working for you, my love, and our Now moments are precious seconds of life.

A massive part of me is crying out in anguish that I am not ready. Why now when we were embarking on a new business together, a new divinely-inspired adventure before us? Our lives' big vision was filled with excitement and anticipation of the beautiful work we were going to share with the world. Now the rug has been pulled out from under our feet. I can't begin to imagine having to say goodbye to this life when so many dreams were ahead, but I also see the body can only take so much physical pain and suffering.

You are a warrior, my love, a spiritual warrior, unlike anyone I have ever known. I learned an appreciation for life I never knew existed before you entered. I am aware of the unique, small moments, the formation of a cloud in the sky, the magic of a swarm of Mayflies, the mystery of a feather blowing in the breeze in perfect rhythm to the music in the background. You opened my eyes and my heart in so many ways, and I will keep that legacy with me until we meet again.

When we call our friends to rush over so you can have your Living Will and Last Will and Testament signed in front of witnesses, your breathing spasms are intense, breath not coming easily, an arduous struggle. We must get those documents signed. The last thing you want is for me to have to call 911 in the event you pass before Hospice is in place. Finishing the Living Will brings relief to both of us, as the document protects your choices.

I text Jozy because I fear you will not live through the night. He comes by, and we find comfort in camping out in the bathroom with you so you can be near the toilet as your nausea shows itself, the coughing of blood and mucous ever-present. Even so, we laugh and talk and have our moments together, the spiritual trio on this death journey. The bathroom visit is our last night of back and forth conversation with you, my love, as talking becomes harder and harder for your body to manage. Jozy leaves, and we are both grateful for our time with him, knowing you may not survive till morning.

It is an excruciating night of watching you rise and fall, several moments of being on the verge of choking to death and then commanding your spirit to wait until Hospice is fully engaged, making it easier for me. I watch you at the brink of passing out, pulling in the strength of the warrior spirit to stave off death. You yell the words, "No, not now! Not this way!" You share with me that someone on your right side is here to escort you, not sure who it is, but you turn to him and yell your desire to go a different way, another time. We both wonder if your grandfather is that being waiting to help you from the other side of the veil. I am in awe, and at the same time fearing this is the end. You are adamant you want to walk, thinking that if you walk, death will not find the door. I enjoy walking with you for hours as you struggle with the side of you that wants breath to stop. We step outside around 2:00 am to see the stars and take in some fresh air. As long as I support you, you can walk. We do not know this is your last time outside, your last time to view the stars. You marvel at the moon as I stand behind you, holding on tight, my face buried in your neck, smelling your skin and kissing you softly. I am sending you loving support the entire time, while I support your weakened body. I sense you are in awe, transfixed by the sheer beauty of the moon, the stars, home.

The Real Deal

One thing was certain: we had no idea how the passage from this life into the next would unfold. We were unsure when it would happen, so I was on high alert and Jack was fully engaged with his body letting go. Because neither of us had actively participated in someone leaving this plane of existence, we followed our instinct and intuitions as much as possible, assessing what we needed to do for us while navigating the uncharted waters of transition. We knew we needed help.

It was a blessing that the Hospice representative came but the paperwork was still in process, so they were not technically engaged with us until the next day. Hospice is an incredible organization that is a nonprofit branch in many hospitals. We were fortunate to have them near. They offered in-hospice care or at-home hospice care. We rushed to get their service in place so Jack could be home for his death journey and not in a hospital. The woman gave us much-needed support and education on what to expect in the last days. This organization was a blessing for me as I was his primary caregiver, the help they could lend greatly appreciated.

In our conversation with the representative, we realized a Living Will was critical to have in place that day. It was a protection for Jack's wishes of no resuscitation or life support in the event he passed before Hospice care was invoked. We quickly found witnesses to Jack's signature. We were all breathing a sigh of relief as he had struggled even to put the pen in hand to sign the paperwork because the spasms took hold.

It was done. One more measure in place. At that point, the moment dictated survival through the night so 911 did not need to be dispatched.

The intensity of watching Jack gasp for air was not something I was prepared to experience. Seeing my love contorted into a struggle for breath, waiting, waiting, waiting for the next inhale to follow, was torture for both of us. Yet I remained by his side, not questioning whether I could do this but hyper-focused on him, his breath, his comfort, ready to jump into action and be with him no matter what transpired.

Jack had a small and blessed reprieve when Jozy came by. We spent time together, laughed about hanging out in the bathroom, and found moments of joy radiating between the three of us. Jack's lightheartedness would catch us off guard and we were so grateful for the bathroom scene. We all commented how crazy this moment would seem to others and we laughed while eating the popsicles Jack insisted we enjoy together.

Jozy left and the rest of the night was a battle for survival until Hospice was in place. The last thing Jack wanted was to have the police called, the coroner brought in, and be carted away by an ambulance. Without Hospice in place, that is the legal process when someone dies at home, at least where we live. With Hospice on board, a person can pass at home with family around. The Hospice nurse is called and works directly with the mortuary. It is a simple process and family and friends are given the time they need to be with their loved one after they pass. It is their call, not that of authorities. That is what Jack wanted me to experience.

The true essence of the human spirit is a wondrous thing to witness. I will never underestimate the power of intention. I watched it over and over again as Jack's body was gasping for air, fighting for the next breath, and with the command of an all-powerful soul, he found the next inhale. He intended to leave peacefully, just pass, not struggling for air. I was his partner through every step that night.

Jack and I both felt spirits around us. Jack yelled at one of them, not ready to give in to death in a traumatic way. He wanted to go on his terms. We could feel the sacred energies around us both; the hair stood up on my skin many times in those hours, signaling powerful energies were present. Were they here to help him leave now? We did not know.

The night air was fresh and cool at 2:00 a.m. and we shared one last walk outside. Nature has such a calming effect on our psyche. We fell into a loving embrace while watching the moon for the last time together. We knew that each of these precious moments was more release of what we had known. We honored the awareness that we shared the magic of our last encounter with the energy of nature, one last enjoyment of the moon's beauty through the tenderness of divine love.

September 19, 2019

My love, you are beginning to pop in and out of this reality, at times lucid and others not here, as you turn inside to what is taking place within your body. I mention I have a question, but then I quickly retract as I know speaking causes spasms and shortness of breath. You motion me to get you the computer. You type, "What is your ?" I respond that I am wondering what is happening when you drift off. "Do you know where you are?" You type, "Short answer is I am working the puzzle most all of the time. Memory is not very good, so in that, present moment is sometimes the only place I can remember very well, if at all. Staying present with the energy, constantly."

I honor that, my love. I will continue to support your process to the best of my ability.

I am so glad Hospice is fully engaged today, and the nurses are here. They are so kind and supportive, and they answer many questions. I believe I am ready for the next step.

But now I sit here watching you once more; this time in so much conflict it breaks my heart. We made a pact that we would work with our energies; we would work to make your passing be one of dignity, in full awareness of the process of transition from this life into that of spirit, you and I in the most profound form of love, letting go. But, while the Hospice nurse is here, you go into one of your breathing spasms,

81

locking up and struggling to breathe into your cancer-filled lungs. We give you medication to help with the pain, medication to help relax your spasm response, medication to ease your anxiety, and medicine to stop your vomiting. Now I gaze over and see you resting better than you have rested in weeks, but I also see a drugged body that is not conscious in a way you had been only a couple of hours ago, so many medications making consciousness elusive.

I am so sorry, my love. I feel my gut wrenching as I send you love through my tears, my awareness you are not alert in the same way even in sleep. Well-meaning intentions have guided you into the complete state of numbness you did not want to experience while not fully understanding the levels of pain a body can endure and remain attached to this plane of existence.

I am so confused as to what to do to help you and honor our pact. Part of me is relieved to see you resting and part of me in anguish, realizing our last in-depth and conscious conversation is now a memory. The warrior in you I have always seen is exhausted from the battle, your resolve depleted by cancer cells running rampant throughout your body. I want you to understand with all of your soul: I am forever connected to you and, more than anything else in this world, I love you enough to say goodbye. My parting gift is for you to feel my release, my acknowledgment of a journey well-traveled, so that you can move into the next adventure without my energetic cords holding you back, only a cloud of compassionate, all-encompassing love surrounding you. God, how it pains me, though! Too fast, way too fast!

Unwavering Commitment

I found myself in awe of the commitment Jack made to his soul's journey, his unquestioned release of life on earth. His dedication to the task at hand was commendable and I could perform no more noble task than to help him achieve that goal. It was now about the continued release of his physical body.

The thing I found so fascinating was that his soul was intact. I saw it, saw through the mind going, the popping in and out. When he had moments of lucidity, his words were poignant. This man was accomplishing the release of his physical body while enduring extreme discomfort and pain. I was grateful for the assistance of the Hospice nurse. We now had access to medications for his comfort.

The double-edged sword was that his level of discomfort required medication that knocked him out, made him unconscious, a zombie-like being, but at least he was resting. A part of me died then. Watching him from my chair next to the bed was excruciating and yet I was grateful for his body's ease, the first time in a couple of months that his cough subsided, the body no longer in spasm. I had to keep reminding myself that, from here on out, it was about physical release. If I were to have moments of clear connection with Jack, it would be a blessing to treasure but not one I could expect.

I began to embrace my release of Jack's physical body in those moments. My innate knowing his soul was alive and well inside that body was absolute, unquestioned. His departure would signal his soul freedom, and the higher awareness in me yearned for that for him.

I cried alone while he lay in bed in a fog of medication. For the first time since his diagnosis, I let my tears flow unbridled. I needed the emotional release. I was becoming exhausted from holding the light and needed to be held by a power greater than myself. I called in my guides and angels. I was calling on all of the beings of light and loved ones who have passed to be there with us in the last days of letting go. The door to other dimensions was beginning to show itself in the energy field and it was tangible. I could feel and sense the beings around us. I felt soothed by them and sensed healing energies flowing around and through me.

I kept to the tasks at hand. I rubbed sacred oils on Jack's swollen feet. His bodily fluids were starting to build in his legs and feet and the skin became tight. While he lay there, I rubbed in his favorite essential oil, patchouli, along with sandalwood, frankincense, and myrrh. Sandalwood is a sacred oil used to connect to the soul, the higher aspect of our being. All of these oils can be used in sacred ceremony. Rubbing oils, with intention, on the feet of one you love expresses the highest honor.

I played the beautiful soothing music with nature scenes 24 hours a day so when he woke, however briefly, Jack would see nature and hear wonderful sounds being played. I used a diffuser to disperse the oil he loved (called Highest Potential) so he would smell the scent that drew him, a scent with which we had both connected when we were falling in love. I made sure all his favorite stones were near; he could see them when he looked over the side of the bed. My picture was on the stand so he could see me with the big trees he loved.

Each of these activities was helping me prepare the stage for Jack to say goodbye. It was part of my gift in letting go of him to offer this beautiful environment so he could leave in peace, whenever that happened.

September 20, 2019

You are now moving into the state of mind of letting go; random thoughts, broken sentences, past images mix with current reality, confusion caused by popping in and out of this reality. I can still talk with you, but my words are repeated several times as you gaze at me, and then you are gone. I pull you back by asking, "Are you ready to take your anti-spasm medication?" You look at me as if it is the first time you have heard that. We repeat that process many times, and what might be a task that would typically take two minutes becomes a task requiring 20 minutes. A trip to the restroom has now become a marathon that may or may not reap results as you stand over the toilet with my help, trying to urinate. You fall asleep while we stand there, and I gently whisper in your ear to remind you again, "Do you think you need to go?" I'm not even sure how much your state of being is related to the body letting go or the medications running through it.

I visit with my mom on the phone. Watching you go is getting so hard, and I sob and cry, not confident I can do this alone anymore. Mom is coming to be with me, to help me through these last days. I need someone else here. I can no longer do this alone with you, my love. I need help so I can be strong support for you. The Hospice nurses are amazing but their visits are once or twice daily. I need full-time back up and mom is more than happy to be my lifeline.

My day is consumed with caring for you and finding moments to take food into my body. I have to keep my strength up; the task at hand demands that of me. I pray. I keep calling in the angels, the guides who are our spiritual support. I am so glad mom will be here in a few short hours. You tell me the purple lights and orbs are all around. At one point, you whisper, "The light beings are here; they are near." I find that whisper brings relief to my hurting heart. My love, many, many people have been praying for you, for us. What else can they do? It is working, and I am so glad you have an awareness of those on the other side who are helping you, preparing you for your journey. I know they are also helping me stay strong of heart and resolve, filling me with love and peace. I am finding moments of clarity and strength within myself I never knew existed. I am having conversations with you, not sure you are hearing me, but encouraging you, connecting to your spirit, reminding you that you are taking this heroic, last step. You know how to do this. You were made for this.

Strange how time warps. I look back at what seems so long ago and then return to the reality that we were in the ER only16 days ago. So much has happened, your every moment changing, your body going through so much turbulence and storm.

I realize you knew a week ago that your journey would not be a miracle in this realm but your ticket home.

Time Becomes One Long Moment

Caring for a loved one while in the process of transition from life to life after death can be exhausting, no matter how strong the resolve or emotional stability of the caregiver. I have viewed much of my life through the lens of energy and I knew my energy reserve was depleting, being drained by lack of sleep, watching Jack release his body, the struggle this process was for him, pulling my energetic ties away from him so he could feel safe to leave. I needed back-up help to deal with the unknown dismantling of the life of my love. I was relieved to know Mom could drop everything and was on the road to be with us.

Being a sensitive, empathic person, I was paying attention to every nuance in Jack's mannerisms, his words, his whispers. The medications had added a level of calm to his body but he was not as coherent, wanting to sleep much of the time. For that, I was grateful. When awake, at times he was clear and intelligible while at other times he seemed to be in another place, another time, another realm.

Jack was tapping into other dimensions and beginning to see and describe things that gave me reassurance. He knew the light beings were around him. Jack had always been a seer. In other words, he had the gift of seeing between the dimensions of reality. Obviously, popping in and out of this third-dimensional matrix was an aptitude that had started early in his life, as mentioned by the Medical Intuitive. He would see orbs in the sky, lights dancing, the energetic grid surrounding earth, spirit beings in another field, and often heard etheric sounds. His seeing and feeling those benevolent, loving energies around him during this time of transition was a comfort to both of us.

Time for me had become a strange mix of fatigue and alertness in moments that stretched and morphed into a no-time zone. I was on the wheel of passage but, like the wheel, time wrapped in, around, and on top of itself. In one long moment, I could replay the entire 16 days as if on a video screen, fast-forwarding to any one moment and hitting freeze frame. Jack was not the only one experiencing a melding and letting go of time. I am sure you have heard that time is relative: relative to your experience and interpretation of it. A part of me wanted to make time stretch, slow it down and have more. Another part of me wished for time to quicken, to not let Jack's suffering linger. Thus, this internal dialogue I was having with aspects of my being was constant, except when I was engaged with assisting Jack.

The Hospice staff brought over a hospital bed to make it easier for Jack to maneuver in and out of bed as he weakened. We set up the bed while Jack watched and visited with the young man assisting. He was moved by Jack's kindness, the gentle nature of a dying man who accepted his journey with grace and appreciation. The nursing staff was taken by his expressions of gratitude for their excellent care while they were with him. They could see it in his eyes, the light still shining.

Gentle mercy for letting go was my request of our divine Source, family of light, the angels who were near. I was not sure how I would be able to move on in life without this gentle, deeply spiritual man who was my soul mate. Help me, I implored!

September 21, 2019

I am relieved one of the medications from Hospice (morphine) is finally helping you with the pain. I also feel blessed when you have moments of clarity, when I know you are present with me in this reality, because those precious times are dwindling.

You can still stand and walk with help, but it is becoming harder; you shuffle, you're growing weaker by the moment. And yet in the morning you want to be in the kitchen with me; we stand next to each other, my body your stabilizer. You start to grind coffee beans. You are clear, lucid. I ask you what you are doing, and you say, "Please let me do this one last time for you. For 12 years, I made the morning coffee and brought it to you in bed. It's my way of treating you special, showing you how much I love you."

You are aware I have to learn to do all of this by myself. You comment, "You are going to realize how much I did around the house and business when I am gone." I laugh and tell you I am already well aware of how much you did and how much I will miss you when you're gone. We smile, the coffee beans ground, and I help you back to bed.

My daughter, Brandee, wants to see you so she drives over from Spokane. She needs to be here for both of us. We lost my ex-husband just three months ago. Now we are losing you, my love. That is a lot to handle, and, while she did not get to say goodbye to her stepfather, she does want to say her goodbyes to you.

It is lovely that another dear friend, Adele, came to stay with you for a while so I can go out to dinner with Mom, Brandee, and granddaughter, Clara. You make me laugh when you motion and say to Adele, "Come join me in bed." You look at me, smile, and say, "We will keep our clothes on." I laugh at you and remark that, at this point, I do not care whether you do or don't keep your clothes on. I smile kindly at you as I mention you have not lost your sense of humor. "Until my dying breath," you say. Those lighter moments are forever burned into my psyche.

Thank you, my love, for welcoming Mom here and for asking her to stay with us. It means a lot to me that she is here during the most challenging task of your transition. It is heartwarming to see you look into Brandee's eyes and tell her she is a very special soul, that you loved her and you made your peace with her. She is so appreciative, and her time on the bed beside you is marvelous to witness, even though you cannot share the popsicle you so wanted with her as it threw you into spasm. One more pleasure was eliminated.

Tonight is not a comfortable night. You are restless, my love, and all I want to do is hold you and calm you. It seems you struggle every hour with some challenges, and sleep is elusive for us both, but I do not care. I just want to comfort you.

Saying Goodbyes

I was in awe of how a simple thing in our life took on an even deeper, more profound meaning. The mundane task of making coffee became a sacred act of love that filled the room with an energy of holiness. Yes, it was a simple gesture, but with the finality of another last act of love. Jack blessed me with a flood of emotion as he reminded me he was leaving, but wanted to care for me in his unique way while he still could. And as usual, the normalcy of his sense of humor, laughing together, was a welcome reprieve to the heaviness of our mission.

This day seemed like a step back into an earlier version of Jack. His body was more comfortable with the assistance of morphine and his mind alert much of the day. It helped to have Mom here. She took up the slack on household duties so my focus could be on Jack completely, wholly. Having a support network is critical while in the death process with a loved one. It is taxing on the caregiver's physical, mental, emotional, and spiritual body. I was happy to accept the help, encouragement, and comfort.

Visits from Hospice nurses went better than expected and again, Jack maintained his sense of humor with them. The young man who brought the bed the day before was the same one to bring oxygen; we all thought the added oxygen might increase his comfort. When I escorted the young man out the door, he remarked that, though he had met many people in his line of work who were in the death process, Jack was unique; he had touched the young man's heart in a way that left a mark like no other. He was taken by Jack's essence, his light, and he was grateful to have met Jack, hoping he would see him again.

In the evening, our dear friend Adele offered to be with Jack so I could get out of the house for a little while with my mom, daughter and granddaughter. The break would do me good and a nice meal would keep up my physical strength. When Adele arrived, Jack was delighted. He loved her and happily sent me out the door. His eyes sparkled with a sense of mischievous delight and I relished this moment of humor and lightheartedness. I was in a state of wonder at his ability to step into his being through the morass of physical detachment. They enjoyed their evening together even though he slept through most of it. When she left, she knew the goodbye was final.

It was such a relief that Brandee made it in time to visit with Jack. My ex-husband had passed away just three months earlier and none of us had the opportunity to say goodbye to him. This time, she was able to find closure. I witnessed a beautiful exchange between them and my heart swelled with an unfathomable love that overshadowed the reason for the visit. Healing for both souls sitting on the bed was tangible and I witnessed a deposit of love-honoring of each other that will always stay with me.

Saying goodbye to a loved one is a gift not always possible. Many people leave this planet quickly, without prior notice. It is a shock to those remaining. We are so tied together in love and emotion, bloodlines and family structures, friendships and work relationships, but we are also linked to our loved ones energetically. There is a cord of energy connecting us to those we love. That cord knows no bounds, exists across time and space. It ties us to them and can be a remarkable or traumatic aspect of the relationship. This is how energy works. It is neither good nor bad; it just is.

When someone transitions from this life, the cord to earthly energy goes with them; it dissipates and is withdrawn, just like Jack's chakra system went from healing green to withdrawal-mode gray. We feel that void, that energy withdrawal. When we have an opportunity to say goodbye, it softens the blow to our field; the cord begins to dissolve through awareness and by choice. The sudden withdrawal can be challenging, like receiving an unwelcome gut punch. But goodbyes can be performed differently, in a way that helps heal the void, even after the person has gone. The remaining energetic ties are of a different vibration, a more divine connection through our light body.

Goodbyes were our healing salve to the releasing of Jack's physical form.

September 22, 2019

I have lost track of time completely. I have surrendered to the Now moments. I feel strange and somewhat numb, my love. You insist on trying to get up to urinate, but your legs no longer hold you. Oh, this is torturous at times! You want to hold your glass of water, and yet your hands no longer grasp. You keep dropping the glass and are irritated with me when I try to help, reminding me of children in tantrum wanting to do it themselves. We already changed your clothes once from spilling the glass of water all over. I feel your frustration with losing your abilities to move, and my heart aches with compassion, bursting in my chest with a pain that seems to grasp me in a stranglehold. My love, you are beginning to lose your grip on this physical reality. All I can do is gently nudge, place my hand under yours, so I can catch it if the glass drops.

The day seems filled with efforts to keep you comfortable. We try several medications to help you with the ever-present spasms; none of them seem to help much, and some alter your personality or make matters even worse with other side effects. That is why I ask the hospice nurse if I can just give you morphine, as it seems to be the only drug that helps your body remain calm and out of the danger zone of spasm, while keeping your awareness more present. Yes, he tells me, I should do what I feel is best for you. My love, I know you cannot talk coherently with me now about what is happening, so I pray I am assisting you in the best way possible, the highest outcome for your comfort.

Around 6:30 pm, I walk into the studio from the kitchen and am shocked to see you sitting bolt upright. You look surprised and ask, "Where is your son? He was just here. Where did he go?" I explain my son is in Idaho right now, and you slowly calm again, confused at what happened because you are so sure he was there. I sit with you, holding your hands as you drift away. Your eyes close again, and a few moments later, you whisper, "Thank you, son." Later I ask my son what he was doing between the time you wondered where he was and when you said thank you. My son says he was hiking a trail in the wilderness of Idaho and was thinking of you, asking you to see through his eyes what he was seeing and experiencing: the beautiful trees, the trail, feeling the wind, surrounded by nature. He wanted you to be with him as he rode the trail. I am so happy you experienced one last trek in the woods, my love.

We finally get some sleep between the medication doses, and Mom watches over you in the early morning so I can rest easier.

What Is Reality

Oh my, this day was hard. There was no way around what Jack's body had to go through to release its hold on life in the physical. I developed a deep gratitude and appreciation this day for all souls who work in Hospice and end-of-life coaching. The letting go continued though, just hours before, Jack was with us with mental clarity. By this time, those moments were fleeting and he seemed to be reverting to a state of basic childlike awareness. Several days earlier, he told me he was working the puzzle, his memory going and present moment the only place he could remember, if at all. Jack had been working the puzzle of his death passage. Detachment, another level of passage, presented itself on this day.

It was as if my Jack was leaving and the body was lagging behind. I patiently waited while dealing with basic needs, such as a sip of water. Holding a glass was a considerable feat that had caused upset when his hands could no longer carry weight, water spilling all over the bed. I gently held the urinal when he felt the urge to pee while I awkwardly kept him propped up on the side of the bed. He wanted to walk to the bathroom but his legs no longer supported him. Through all the physical letting go, I held compassion for the journey my love was taking, continuously encouraging him along the way, seeing how much courage these last steps required.

I became awash in a surreal landscape of maintaining Jack's comfort and feeling the sacred nature of what was taking place. Leaving the body is a hero's journey and I became acutely aware of all those leaving the planet, realizing how heroic we all are with the level of courage it takes to let go of the physical body.

It was a blessed reprieve when Jack rested because his physical discomfort was on the rise again. I realized some of the medicines used to help him deal with the shut-down caused other unnecessary physical side effects. He had enough challenge and, with his Hospice teams support, I reduced his medications, the morphine being the only one helping him now.

Brandee and Clara had gone home after a teary goodbye. Mom and I were fixing dinner for ourselves while Jack was sleeping when I heard something. I went into the studio to see him sitting at the edge of the bed, eyes wide open. This level of alertness was something I had not seen from him for many hours so I was surprised. That is when he asked where my son was. He had just seen him so he was confused. I could have just marked it up to the mind going away, but his thank you to my son was genuine. I felt his gratitude penetrate my heart and knew it was something more. When my son validated the timing and what he had been doing at that same moment, there was no doubt. Jack had experienced one more time in nature. Does that mean I believe he traveled with his etheric body to see what my son shared with him? Absolutely! We are multidimensional beings having a human experience. The physical body is just a temporary house to Spirit and we have the ability to astral travel to other places, times, and dimensions through intention.

What a wondrous gift for Jack to have one last moment in the natural world he loved so much as seen through my son's eyes.

September 23, 2019

Mom is startled when, out of the blue, you stand up. She is watching you for a few minutes while I wrestle with something in the kitchen and then get ready to take a quick shower. "Becki! Becki! Come here!" she exclaims. I dash into the studio and see you wavering with mom supporting you. You are trying to go somewhere. Mom and I maneuver you around and get you seated on the edge of the bed, but it is not easy as your body seems stiff, as if the muscles are frozen, not wanting to move. I am shocked at your strength in a body that can barely support itself.

My love, seems the lights are dimming and your eyes are beginning to glaze, yet you still sit and connect with me. It is around 9 am, and I am sitting at the edge of the bed with you, holding your magnificent hands that now have no strength. Your head rolls back a little and then, as if startled, you look at me with eyes wide open and say, "Oh my, I need to say goodbye to you now. Becki, I love you!" Then you shakily lean toward me to kiss me one last conscious time. I kiss you back, sobbing in your arms, and share how much I love you too. This exchange is the last time we talk. I realize you stood up to find me and say those precious words that will never leave my soul. You are an amazingly strong and loving man, and our love is so powerful it transcended the physical realm, your soul signaling the goodbye.

By mid-afternoon, you are no longer responsive. When I lift your arm, it just falls back to the mattress, with no muscle activity whatsoever. Your body no longer moves other than to breathe, your heart beating rapidly, your body heat extremely high. I talk to you as I know you can still hear me, even though you cannot respond. I encourage you. You are a warrior, my love. You can move into the next experience, the next life with ease and peace. I say the words while part of me is wilting, dying on the vine.

Jozy comes by to see you and plays his original song on your guitar, Angel, the song the two of you jammed with only a few short weeks ago. It is a beautiful gift, and I see the slight movement of an eyebrow while he plays for you. I know you are hearing him. An exquisite exchange takes place between the two of you. Mom captures him in video playing so we at least have that moment to hold, to remember.

Tonight, you rest. You are now in another realm, another reality only you can know, one I watch from afar. I know we are getting close to your transition, but you had mentioned Wednesday a couple of times in a way that made me wonder if it was to be the day. You had said, "Monday will reveal, Tuesday will expose, and Wednesday will respond." It was cryptic and made me wonder. When we kissed goodbye for the last time, you whispered the word Wednesday. My thoughts circle on how many hours are left now. Will it be Wednesday, or will it be sooner?

I sleep next to you with my alarm set for every two hours so I can check on you and make you comfortable. Your chest rattles and I start giving you the medicine to help relieve somewhat; your breath is not quite so labored.

Final Words

I do not have the words to do justice to Jack's magical and heartbreaking moment shared with me. I hope the energy transcends the page, that readers feel the heart-opening experience of a divine love shared in the most devoted of ways. His last words spoke, a verbal goodbye and one last intimate kiss from the man who loved me beyond time and space. He always told me he thought I was the most beautiful woman on the planet and he felt blessed we were together again. His soul found a way to signal me, find me, so that his last verbal exchange could be branded onto my heart and his last kiss felt on my lips to cherish for as long as I remain on the planet.

"Oh my, I need to say goodbye to you now. Becki, I love you!"

Some moments in life define you, become part of your expression from that moment forward. For me, this defining moment forever changed me. I somehow knew this would become the strength I could hold; it would help me keep going on without him. I knew beyond any doubt that our love was sacred, divine, and more than this earthly expression. He gifted me immeasurably at that moment.

It was only a short time later that his body was no longer responsive.

One more passage had happened. Now Jack's body was completely still, no longer responding with spasms, coughing, flinching, hiccups, or talking; he was just breathing, his heart beating rapidly. I knew he could still hear me. Doctors and nurses say hearing is one of the last senses to leave; the person in a body unable to move is often still present and aware of sound.

So I talk, having a one-sided conversation with Jack. I share my love, encourage him on his journey. I rub essential oils on his feet, legs, arms, and hands as I shower his body with Reiki and love. I know an aspect of him is still feeling me, loving me from the in-between worlds.

Jozy playing a song on Jack's guitar Angel is a beautiful exchange of the love and adoration between friends. I knew Jack could hear him and, when his eyebrow raised slightly, we all knew he was signaling Jozy a thank you for one last song.

I sat back and watched Jack breathe, in and out, in and out, the rhythm mesmerizing and comforting my weary soul. I was tired, wanting for his sake the rest of the passage to go quickly, but not sure of the timing. I was told no one could predict how long a person will take to make their final death passage. It is up to the soul leaving. And so I wait, I cry, I rest, I take care of Jack, I cry, I take care of me, I talk to my mom, I cry. I know it is okay for me to release my emotions. Life since September 4 has been intense, gut-wrenching, and life-altering.

September 24, 2019

My love, you have gone four hours this morning without signs of distress. You seem to be resting, but your breathing has shifted. I have become vigilant in listening to the nuances of the in and out rhythm of your life. Your breath is all I have left, the part of you that reminds me you are still of this world.

The most important job of my life is to help you continue letting go. The body holds on tight. It has a fantastic mechanism for survival. We talked about that. My love, you commented you would go down fighting all the way. You are succeeding. But I implore you now; you do not have to fight anymore; you can move peacefully into the night, knowing full well you have earned the right to peace. You have been an enormous pillar of healing for so many along the way. Your love of music, sound, and beauty, the essence of who you are, has been passed along and will not be forgotten. There are those of us who carry that forward in our unique ways, you forever leaving an indelible mark on our souls.

My love, in this transition from physical form to spirit, you will find freedom, an energy that has always meant so much to you: freedom from your pain and suffering, from the density of the earthly body, from this third-dimensional matrix. The divine is an energy I wish for you, one with which you are so connected. Please set your spirit free. I can't imagine feeling any greater love in this precious life than I do for you at this moment, and yet I set you free.

As I say these words, I know it is time to prepare the altar for you. It will hold sacred items: rocks, crystals, the Warrior's Prayer, your jewelry, guitar picks, a candle, your favorite oils, all going onto your altar for the honor of passage, a celebration into the next expression. The stage is being set.

I play a song that has meant so much to you. I often watched you listen, totally absorbed by the music, tears running down your cheeks as your tender heart was taken away by the sheer power of love, beautiful music, and the incredible message shared. You have always told me you wanted this song played if you should pass. I was not in any position emotionally to play this song for you, but I wanted to get it cued so it would be ready. I find the song on your phone, plug in the speaker, and turn it on to do a soundcheck. I turn it off after the first measure. The sound is sufficient. But then something comes over me and I have a powerful urge to go ahead and play it. My tears are flowing, and I sing along the best I can in tribute to you, a melody that touches the very essence of you. The song finishes, and your breath shifts. Your eyes open. I look at Mom and say, "Oh my gosh, I think he is going!"

I rush over to your side, my love, and caress you, caress your face, tell you how much I love you, and encourage you to go with your family of light, those

107

present to help you. You gaze up past me toward the ceiling as I touch you, crying, placing my hand on your heart as it beats its last beat. Your breath stops, and all is still. Your physical form is silent. I hold you and sob tears of sorrow for my profound, agonizing loss and yet feel relief for your freedom from suffering. You made it, my love, you are free! And you made it happen quietly, peacefully, no gasping or struggle, just sleep: the way you hoped it would be, the way your silent spiritual warrior wanted.

I touch your still body, rubbing your favorite oils on your neck, arms, chest, legs, and feet. I caress your hands that have given me so much tenderness, love, and beautiful music over the years. I embrace you some more, crying my goodbye to your physical form. I ask Mom to help me cut your ponytail. Your hair was always so important to you, an expression of your rebel side. You liked to call yourself the fringe dweller. Together we lift you and I clip your ponytail. It feels important for me to keep that part of you with me, perhaps giving me the strength of the rebel fringe dweller too. I will need to learn to be the guard dog for myself now that you are not here on this plane of existence.

I know you will never be far, that you have just taken off your earthly bodysuit and unmasked your soul. I will find you in the feather blowing in the wind, the cloud formations in the sky, the beautiful music I hear that brings me to tears. You will be there. I will carry on our work in the world with honor and a greater appreciation than I have ever had. As I read this going-away love letter to you, remember it is a goodbye from the physical body only, from the most profound sense of love I can offer. I hold in my heart that, while I will miss this life with you on earth, we are never far apart; you are but a whisper away, always near. Fly on the wings of Spirit, my love. Embrace this new journey. I will see you soon! I am forever yours, my love!

The Final Passage

This passage of the book is being written on the one-year anniversary of Jack's leaving this earth. As I remember this day, read and transcribe my love letter diary to Jack, I am awestruck between the flow of my tears. The day of Jack's death has become part of me, part of my soul in so many ways.

The absolute heartbreak is real and has never left my awareness. It is okay. It is a part of me and I allow my body to feel it, honor it, and let it move through. The blissful joy is absolutely real. I am filled with love and admiration for the soul connection we shared and the death journey we walked together.

On the day of final passage, I set the stage for Jack, holding the most unconditional love and acceptance I was capable of attaining. He could no longer share his needs with me so I watched him, paid attention to his breath, the sounds coming from his mouth. I tapped into the intuitive connection we often laughed about, reading each other's minds and trying to figure out who thought the thought first before one of us voiced it. I was on my own as his body continued to release.

I encouraged him, knowing hearing is one of the last senses to go. I played music for him. Nature scenes were revolving on the television in front of him, not that I expected him to miraculously open his eyes and see them but for my comfort as I sat with the stillness of a body no longer responding. I needed those magnificent Earth images to remind me of beauty.

Mom was here to help me break the hyper-vigilant obsession with his breath; I was so blessed to have her share this with me, this day of my ultimate letting go. She knew my heartache; we had lost Dad four years earlier. Losing her beloved was still raw for her too, but her love for me held a pillar of strength I sorely needed.

And I wrote. I was writing my love letter to Jack. I had read him the diary of our journey from a few days earlier while he could still understand me. He was happy I was displaying my affection for him while on this intense death path. Writing was something he always encouraged me to do. In fact, he knew I would be writing a book about what we were doing, the process we shared. This time was different. I was reading the words written from a heart that recognized Jack would hear me from a soul place; no physical response would follow my voice, no smile of acknowledgment or sparkle in his beautiful blue eyes. Writing has always been a way I transmute; I alchemize what I feel through the written word. Writing would be my task now, more than ever before.

I drew on my wisdom as an energy healer, a person who understands energy knows no bounds, cannot be destroyed, simply changes form. I knew my relationship would move forward in some fashion and had complete faith in the never-ending soul journey we all travel continuing on a beautiful trajectory. Life and death are flip sides of the same coin. Jack had played the lottery and won his trip back home.

After his last breath and my sobbing took a break, I looked at Mom and asked if she had seen any light. I have heard many people see a light as the soul leaves the body. Neither of us noticed any change and then we both had an aha moment. The energy created in the studio throughout Jack's death process was sacred. It was already holding the light of ascension, light beings already present. We knew he was with loved ones and we felt them.

When he passed and I finished my love letter to him, I read it to him. I felt he could hear me from his vantage point in spirit form, not knowing where he was exactly but it felt close, divine. I spent several hours with Jack. Our friend Adele came over to be with us. The three of us held vigil while I felt into my goodbye to Jack's body, allowing myself the time I needed to feel complete with his form.

When the hospice nurse and man from the mortuary arrived, they were in awe of what they saw and felt. The whole room smelled of sacred oils, music was playing, and the television was scrolling beautiful nature scenes. Jack's altar was nearby with his special items, stones were all around the room, and the three of us women were radiating love from our hearts. We were holding space for the man who was the love of my life, the man who had made the heroic journey home, the man who forever changed my life.

Part 2 - Afterlife Connection

I have no regrets

For the love I have for you

Has no boundaries, it is pure

Take my hand and fly

Take my hand and love

Join me in this journey

That has no beginning

And has no end

Where

Time

Stands

Still

My Beloved Jack, 2007

Love Letter to Becki

October - **First Contact**

"You thought I couldn't get any closer to you. Well, I am. I will never leave your side!"

Jack, October 28

Numb! A numb shock took place after Jack passed and, for several days, I felt my body in motion but very little attachment to the form in which I found my soul. I did what needed to be done: Cremation, paperwork, getting the 4-Runner ready to sell, a spattering of Reiki and HeartMath clients, and visits from friends offering condolences. My life was a mixed bag and the automatic pilot was in charge.

I spent the first part of the month traveling with my mom to watch our granddaughters so my daughter and son-in-law could attend a long-planned work trip. The girls, ages five and two, fed my soul with sweet, innocent love. The five-year-old found me in tears a few times and would come and hug me, concerned for my sadness. She understood at some level that Jack was gone and said she missed him too. Mom provided much-needed support as my exhaustion reared its head; I just needed to be in the moment, with the emotions that rose. All my girls were giving me so much love at the time when I needed it most; my heart ripped open and raw, exhausted from the journey.

When I returned home, I invited our friend Jozy to come over for a meditation. I felt a strong pull to give myself a cleansing journey into myself, into my body, into my own divine spiritual realm. I was aware my numb state was wearing off and wanted to move forward in my healing process. I had no expectation or thought of connecting with Jack. I was just relaxing into my body, mind, and spirit.

Jozy and I started with breathwork, deeply grounding our awareness into our heart chakras, breathing in and out of the heart space, pulling in the feeling of love and compassion. I gently guided us into meditation and then went silently into my own experience.

I found myself walking down a beautiful path surrounded by large green trees swaying in a slight breeze. I could smell the ocean air and, as I rounded a bend, I saw an ocean covered and shimmering with flames of gold, red, and orange. The light radiating off the ocean was brilliant and it called to me. I walked forward onto the ocean surface, surrounded by flames lapping up around my body, engulfing me. They were not hot but felt invitingly calm and warm. My heart was peaceful and I rested into the beauty all around. As I gazed over the golden ocean's surface, I saw a figure walking toward me. It was hazy and indistinguishable at first, but as it came close, I could see it was Jack emerging from the bright light, as though the sun was behind him. When I realized it was Jack, I felt a breathtaking energy rush through my body. He was radiant, his eyes sparkling. He scooped me up into his arms and swung me around in total exhilaration, smiling and laughing. I heard him say, "Hi, my love. Thank you for connecting with me, for making an effort to meet me here in this field of awareness, this frequency."

Jack was so happy to see me in this magnificent place. He was encouraging me, telling me I could do this, meet him in this energetic field of connection. "This is how we are going to communicate; this is how we do it now." His joy radiated out of every part of his soul. We held each other in that place of love, hope, and connection. He encouraged me again, "You know how to do this, my love. Remember how to do this. This is our journey." I was enveloped in a divine love; I felt the sacred essence of Spirit. The light of his soul was so joyful it filled me with a state of bliss in that illumination. "This is real," he reminded me. "Meet me here."

I came out of the meditation with my heart open, tears of gratitude flowing down my cheeks. I would never doubt the beauty of Jack's state of being. It was absolutely blissful. His face showed so much compassionate love for me, I knew, with every fiber of my being, we had made first contact.

I went back to work, needing to occupy my mind and augment my income after 40 days of not earning. The ranch work was good for me, part-time gardening in a stunning region of the Montana landscape. So, I went about the duties of fall garlic planting, garden clean-up, and readying garden beds for winter. It was a good distraction, the land healing my soul.

I have always had a strong connection to Earth but a more fitting description for me is Gaia, a term used to describe the living earth. Nature often calls to those who are empathic, people sensitive to energies around them. Nature provides calming respite for the weary soul and the healing effects of nature are real, tangible, and scientifically proven. I was no exception. It was great to breathe in the crisp, fresh air and work with my hands in the soil.

But guess what? Life moves forward in waves and the grief of my loss came crashing down around me on October 28. I struggled to maintain my composure. The day was stormy and a blizzard moved into the valley. By the end of the day, while driving home in a whiteout, I was crying, feeling my gut wrenching, when I saw an eagle in a tree next to the road. I stopped the car and rolled my window down, despite the wind whipping snow inside.

Jack had an affinity for birds but especially for eagles. We had participated in a golden eagle rescue five years earlier. Jack spent three days on a hillside in blizzard conditions with the injured bird while arrangements were made. He did not want her to be taken by wolves. She and Jack had a conversation, a telepathic animal communication, and she told him to call her "aria" (lower case 'a' was specified). After the rescue, she did not live through the night, her injuries beyond her ability to overcome. Jack was like that. I witnessed him at the wildlife rehabber's place the day after the rescue. She called to let us know a bald eagle was there and invited us to meet him. When we arrived, the eagle was

117

very sick in his cage, waiting to head to a veterinarian. The massive eagle's head was cast down, a classic sign of lead poisoning. Jack stood near the cage, offering his heartfelt connection to the majestic bird. His eyes, only inches away, were fixed on that bird and, after several moments, the eagle raised his head slowly and gazed right into Jack's eyes. The hair stood up on my body as I watched an energy exchange take place between man and bird that there are no words to describe, just pure soul to soul compassion.

That is why I stopped when I saw the bald eagle perched in the tree. I had doubted my connection to Jack, feeling as though my grief was somehow blocking me from being able to reach him again. So I did what felt natural, rolled the window down and talked to the bird. The eagle looked at me. He did not move, just kept staring at me. I was there for what seemed a long time but was probably only minutes. I asked the eagle if he was a sign from Jack. I had been imploring Jack only minutes before, crying that I did not trust my connection, asking him to help me.

The eagle just kept looking at me and I knew. My body became electrified and chills ran up and down my spine; no, not due to the cold blowing in the window. These chills were different, like the recognition of a prayer answered. The eagle remained still despite the proximity of my car. I finally became aware of the cold from the snow and had my answer; Jack was near.

The drive home was in extreme blizzard conditions but I felt a calm and deep gratitude for recognizing his sign.

We are given signals all the time from those in the other dimensions: synchronistic numbers seen repeatedly, a unique animal encounter, a found object bizarrely related to the person, place, or thing we had been contemplating. Signals happen in so many ways: in cloud formations we see in the sky, in other people who have just what we seek or say just what we need to hear, a particular song coming on the radio as we are thinking of a special someone. Magic is all around us. It is only a matter of being aware. We are all connected to this phenomenal field of energy and I was learning to trust my multidimensional abilities of discernment.

That night, Lorie Ladd, an ascension teacher and multidimensional channel, was resting into her regular nightly routine of relaxation on her couch when Jack came through with a message. Jack had found Lorie's work in 2018 and we both enjoyed her offerings and we became friends.

He wanted me to let you know that, yes, it's him. It's him you hear. He's really there with you and it's actually him you're hearing. I'm not sure whether you're having doubts around what you're hearing but he's telling me to tell you, Yes! It's him! All of it! And to follow his guidance. Follow what he's telling you or sharing with you. He says this is when it's going to get good. He's calling you Baby. He's sorry he left the way he did but he's right by your side. Even more than before.

"You thought I couldn't get any closer to you," he says. "Well, I am. I will never leave you. Ask and I'll show you. It's all yours," he says.

I'm not sure what he means, but he's communicating all the time with you. Your relationship has just shifted to different dimensional fields.

He's saying, "Let's go. I'm ready."

I'm not sure for what, but he's ready.

I read this message upon awakening in the morning. I cried tears of joy as I knew this was the validation I had been requesting from him. I had no idea it would come through someone else but I could not deny he was connecting with me.

That morning was a chilly two degrees (F) at the ranch and I was in the greenhouse tending to the herbs and flowers that had survived the night. While I worked, I talked to Jack, sure he could hear me. A large flock of snow geese flew over the top of the greenhouse and I said to Jack, "Let's go outside, my love, and see the geese." I grabbed my phone to take a video of the spectacular sight. The air was crisp and the backdrop of the blue sky was stunning.

I shot three videos of the geese flying overhead, with their cacophony of sound in the background but did not think too much more about it as I continued my workday. When I got home that night, I looked at the video footage and was blown away by what my camera had captured. All three videos were taken only seconds apart in the same environment, but the first video was extraordinary. A beautiful orb of light danced across the scene, up and around the birds, then in front of the sun with a big flare, and finally it slowly danced off the screen. I knew Jack was showing me he was with me; he went out with me to see the geese and give me a visible sign he was near. "Ask and I'll show you," took on a whole new meaning. The veil between our dimensions was non-existent at that moment.

I guess I needed reassurance my intuitions and impressions were not just my wishful thinking. While I believe that can happen, what happens more often is we discount the validity of our ability to transcend dimensional fields of awareness. We second-guess ourselves in an attempt to make sense of intuitive information we receive. All the while, it may very well be a loved one or a guide who is nudging us to pay attention, listen with soft ears, see with subdued vision, feel with imagination to the whisper of their energy.

And then again, contact from another soul or guide may be blatant and in our face. Accept it all because we're remembering how to use our sixth sense again, our intuitive eyes becoming clearer the more we let go of judgment and disbelief.

In the midst of missing Jack, in my extreme human grief, I experienced the magic of life after life. Jack was doing his best to let me know he was near and contact would continue, our journey together not done.

Jack's Message

> *My love, first, I want to thank you for taking this passage journey with me. It took courage, vulnerability, and opening to the uncertain future ahead of you. I am so happy you remembered: remembered me, us, our love, our contract. Thank you.*

> *It is with great honor and excitement that I get to share with all who read or are touched by our book.*

> *It is not always easy or quick for a soul to go through the passage and emerge in the place I found myself right away. But I did the work; **we** did the work of my passage together. I let go of my baggage and arrived free, ready to do my work here, from my new*

realm. It is not always that way. It was easier for me in my transition because I had let go of human life completely. I never let go of love; I reside in a state of high-vibrational, all-encompassing love. It is the driving force that animates everything around me.

There are souls who need time, who go into healing before developing the ability and opportunity to connect to those still in the physical plane. Some feel confused, not sure where to go or how to get here, especially when passing is sudden, unexpected. The more we can help people accept death as a beautiful part of life, the easier transition will be for the soul. Life is magnificent from this place, the human exchange only a blip on the radar of no-time. Where I am is eternal, real, and who we truly are. Many of us as souls support our loved ones left on the Earth plane and many other aspects of our work support humanity and the planet as a whole.

We, as souls in light body and you as humans, have the ability and opportunity to connect. I am able to connect with you, my love, because I was ready to come back right away, having already set the stage through the conscious death process we accomplished. We are fulfilling what we came to do: share with others the ability to move beyond the dimensions of time and space, reminding humans who they truly are as light and love. There are no barriers in our ability to communicate. It is a matter of attunement to each other. Keep dialing in. Many of us souls, are ready and waiting, supported by legions of angels, light beings, and galactic families.

My love, thank you for sharing this.

November - Psychic Ability Expands

"Thank you for holding my hand through the death process."
Jack, November 1

I learned to allow my feelings to come up, my tears to flow. And I took steps to continue my newfound connection. Jack had said to me, this is where we meet, this field of the in-between, and in order for me to access that field, I meditated. It seemed to work before and I tested the waters, dipping my toes in this newfound ability to tap into the higher dimensional field of Spirit.

Jozy came by and we went into another meditation. We started with breathing into our bodies, feeling our heart-breath as we grounded into the body, at the same time feeling the energy rise. During the meditation, I traveled down the familiar path through a forest of dense trees on one side and a beautiful meadow on the other. As I was strolling down the path, I gazed up at the branches on the pines and all of a sudden, Jack popped out from behind a tree into the path in front of me. The sun was shining behind him and he was smiling from ear-to-ear. His face was beaming and he was excited to see me. I was happily shocked and said to him, "Wow, that was fast. How are you?"

He smiled at me and encouraged me to walk the path with him toward the ocean. I was ecstatic to be with him and we walked together until we reached the beach. This beach is a familiar site and Jack said to me, "Yes, we are together here. Yes, you are hearing me. Yes, we are connected. I want you to look out over the ocean and see what I see."

I looked out over the ocean and was astonished to see angels, thousands and thousands of angels for as far as my eyes could see, floating above the water. He said to me, "See, they are here, they are all here supporting you. They are here to help you, to help us. Becki, let them fill you. Feel your heart. Feel the love they have for you. Let it absorb into your soul."

When he said that, I allowed my heart to feel into what the angels were sending. A huge rush of energy entered my heart center and I felt my body vibrating. I started crying as the energy was such a powerfully beautiful, divine light and my heart expanded beyond anything I had felt before previously.

I started to converse with Jack. I asked, "Am I really feeling you Jack? Am I really talking to you? Am I channeling you?"

He said, "Yes. Pay attention and keep working; keep doing what you are doing."

I questioned him because I kept hearing his words in my own voice. Hearing my voice confused me, caused me to doubt.

How could I really know it is not just my mind playing tricks with me? He said, "If you need to hear me in my voice, go back to my videos, my recordings, and listen; remember my voice. You can hear me in my voice. If that will help you, go to that place of memory of my voice."

This whole time we had been standing. Then Jack guided me to lie on the beach with him, watching the waves of the ocean rise and fall. He reminded me Jozy needed support too, that I could help him with his journey. He then suggested I send Jozy energy from my heart to his heart. As I started to send energy to Jozy's heart from mine, Jack joined in and also sent loving energy, amplifying the beam of love. It was an incredible wave of energy between Jack and me, blending into one beautiful wave into our dear friend's heart chakra.

Jack and I then walked back to the trail and, next to the path, we sat at the base of a tree with our backs against the warm, fragrant bark. He encouraged me to keep doing the work of connecting. He told me the more I practiced coming into this awareness, the easier it would be to access him. He gently reminded me to keep trusting this is real, our connection is not gone.

I finished the meditation absorbed in a feeling of complete joy and lightness of heart. This experience was my first indication Jack and I would still be working together in the energetic field, the multidimensional field of awareness. I had no idea where it was going to go. All I knew was it was my task to just keep open and alert, allowing the energy to flow.

I continued to work with meditation in order to expand my trust in my ability to connect with and channel Jack, along with this new-found psychic awareness. My intuition became even stronger and, at the same time, I rode waves of grief and loss, knowing the waves were part of the process and it was all okay.

Another dear friend, Sherry, a hypnotherapist and life coach, made contact with me after hearing Jack had passed. She wanted to use her skills to support me during my time of grief. We set up an online conference call to renew our connection. I gave her a little background on the events taking place since Jack left, filling in the blanks, so to speak. We had anticipated maybe doing some hypnotherapy or grief counseling.

All of a sudden Jack came through to her. Unbeknownst to me, she was also a spirit medium who was not practicing that skill at the time but working with more traditional counseling. She was as surprised as I was when she exclaimed, "Oh my gosh, Jack is here. He's talking to me. Well, I guess this is where we are going to go, talking to Jack!"

Jack told her I was absolutely on the right track and that there were so many beings supporting us, the angelic realm very strong. She mentioned the angelic realm was huge around Jack and me. Jack also said through her, "Thank you for holding my hand through the death process. I love you, Becki. We will be doing this work together. What we have to share is needed in the world. The angels are with us. Keep moving forward and trusting."

Sherry and I discussed the idea of sharing the conscious death journey with others, what that experience might be like on my end. I was feeling blessed but overwhelmed. I had no idea what my "new work" would look like or how it would be executed.

Sherry has always had the gift of mediumship, communicating with souls on the other side, and worked in that field for many years, even though she was also practicing more traditional counseling. She shared with me that there are angelic beings on the other side whose job is to assist souls who have left the physical form, a type of re-entry support and soul mending that is part of passage from the physical realm of existence into the spiritual realm of existence. Some souls pass suddenly and can be confused about where they are. Others are deeply emotionally wounded when they pass and need healing support. She told me these angelic teams were the ones most excited about the work Jack and I were doing together, the conscious death process and afterlife connection so many others can experience. Jack's soul was quickly able to come back and work with me, his emotional healing done before he passed, performed together in a deep and abiding love of letting go into the next version of soul expression.

I was so grateful he had come through to someone else. He was obviously hard at work on his side of the veil.

At the end of November, a friend and I held a Reiki training class. We are both master teachers and as such, we often train others in this beautiful energy-healing practice. I was getting used to meditations where Jack and I connected. This weekend was no exception.

I found myself at the familiar location on the calming and beautiful beach near the ocean in meditation. As I was sitting there, I looked out and saw dolphins playing in the waves in front of me. Jack came and sat down next to me and we watched the dolphins. He reminded me to keep listening to the subtle realm that he was with me all the time. We watched the dolphins for a little while longer and he suggested I give my own heart Reiki energy, that I place my hands on my heart. When my hands were there, he put his hands on top of mine. I felt a deep sense of peace move through me and we sat together at that moment, completely content.

I am aware that not everyone thinks they have the ability to visualize with clarity in meditation. I started my meditation journey with the same thought: I don't see in my mind's eye very well, if at all. My third eye, intuitive vision, seemed blocked. But somewhere along the way, I found the awareness to let go and allow whatever happens to happen. I stopped trying to see and visualize and just dropped into my body and my breath. The exciting result was that, at some point, I started seeing images in my mind's eye. I am not even sure I am aware of when it began to happen. It was as if one day I just realized an image appeared. What I knew for sure was I was feeling into my body, into my breath.

Jack was great at meditation and it was a practice we enjoyed together, often sharing insights into the experience. Now, that was the energetic field where we could meet. A part of me was beginning to understand what he knew before he passed: that this would take place, the evolving of our relationship into a divine connection which was not leaving, our work just beginning. He was ready! I continued to learn to trust.

Jack's Message

My love, I honor your courage to move beyond thinking-mind into the higher awareness states where we can meet. Meditation has been a key.

All who read, when you meditate, it helps your body's own energetic frequency rise. The more you rise, the closer we (those in spirit) are. We can move closer to you but it is much easier if you assist and meet half-way. It is in the in-between that my love and I meet. That is the communing of our souls. This will become more and more accessible as humanity ascends, rises into the destined higher-vibrational evolution.

The life and death process will be seen as a beautiful passage, an initiation into our freedom, expansion, full light. Humans are still in so much fear, fear keeping the channel clogged, not as open. Trust is a part of the opening, the turn of the valve so energy can flow. So many souls are ready to be received, wanting to assist humanity in remembering who they are, divine essence never ending.

It is okay. Be gentle. We are here with you no matter whether you feel us. I am with many souls in this divine place, helping people remember their ability to connect, to channel communication. It is all okay, in perfect time. Do what feels right to help you remember who you are, whether it is meditation, music, dance, writing, laughter. It matters not what you use. I used music while there to open the door of dimension for me. I still have music here; it is infused in my being. I still carry an aspect of me, my personality, my sense of humor. We want you to realize you will recognize us when you open to your gift to hear Spirit. There is nothing to fear. Trust. We send signals all the time.

My love, thank you for trusting.

December - Enter Other Spirits

"Feel into me. Feel the coolness of me near. I am never not near you. Death is what we came to do, our journey together. I am holding an energetic portal open between my world, the in-between world, and your world."

Jack, December 31

December found me opening the calendar to schedule my regular Reiki clients again, feeling more stable in my emotional stability and ready to serve others. I was becoming accustomed to feeling Jack. Many encounters continued to validate the channel opening between us, like a radio dial finding the sweet spot for clear reception. I became familiar with his energy field, learning to feel when he was near, listening for his messages. I was walking into untrodden territory. I have always been in awe of people who have the gift of "sight," those who tap into realms of multi-dimensional reality. Never did I suspect I would be saying to anyone that I was talking to the spirit of my beloved who died. I was finding myself in vulnerability as much as I was excited to explore. It takes courage to step into a completely new reality and share aspects of life with other people not easily explained and often judged.

The real test came when I gave a Reiki session to a client I had not seen since before Jack transitioned. I had no idea his daughter had passed away just a week after Jack. When he came into the healing studio, we shared some lovely moments of understanding, of heartfelt love connection through loss.

The session began as always; I focused and allowed while the healing Reiki energy flowed where it would serve the person for their highest need and greatest purpose. I was used to feeling Jack around me, often aware of his support, but I always held that knowledge to myself, not verbalizing it with most other people. All of a sudden, I heard a female voice speaking, faint but clearly not Jack. This was a new experience and I wondered what to do, nervous about saying anything to my client. But, at her continued insistence, I told him what she was asking me to share with her father. Tears of joy erupted from him; it was precisely what he needed to hear. He then told me he had known she would make contact with me; he just felt it. My lesson was an even deeper level of vulnerability and trust.

The unexpected was taking place. Other souls who were related to the person on the table started coming to me in session. Not only other souls but higher consciousness beings and guides were beginning to arrive. I was learning to accept this new form of mediumship while my work evolved.

The next time Jozy and I got together to meditate we both had a strange time warp sensation. When the session was over, we felt as if it had only been five minutes and it had been a full 30 minutes. I also experienced multidimensional reality playing out an entire scene where time stood still. I found myself at the ocean, this time standing at the top of a rocky bluff overlooking the vast expanse of water. The wind was blowing and I was wearing a long, flowing, white gown and my long hair blew wildly around me. This scenario is familiar to me as I have been here many times before. I saw Jack in the distance walking along the beach. I motioned for him to join me and he was immediately there, a part of me confused as to how he arrived so fast. He was standing on the rocky bluff with me while we looked out over the ocean together. We then sat down and had a discussion about our work. When I asked him for clarity about something Lorie had mentioned in October, my body was immediately filled with knowing the answer and chills enveloped me.

Lorie and I had both wondered what he meant when he said, "It's all yours."

Energy poured into my heart as I recognized what he meant. I literally embodied all of him, to the depth and breadth of his soul. I was breathing in that moment of energy exchange and he smiled with acknowledgment of my remembrance. We were one. Our souls shared a combined essence and I knew what he meant without words, an internal knowing, as if our thoughts were of one mind. I had access to all of him in his afterlife.

When I came out of the meditation, I was awash in the energy of love and, although it seemed like a short 5-minute session, I radiated peace.

The more I learned to trust Jack, our connection and communication, the more mediumship and psychic information started to flow. It was as though Jack was at the gate (a type of portal between dimensions) opening the door for spirits and guides to come to me. We often joked about how he was my guard dog, patrolling the periphery of my energy field, protecting it because I tended to be so open. He kept the strays at bay in life. It made sense that he was still somehow helping me learn this newfound skill with support and protection, but I had to continue doing my part.

Kris, another new client, came to the healing center for Reiki and her daughter, Liberty, who had passed 2 ½ years earlier, came to her while in session, providing further opportunity for me to walk into trust and allow the information to flow. I honored the spirits who were coming through with messages; I felt blessed to be a medium of connection for departed loved ones.

Our friend Adele came in for a couple of Reiki sessions. She already felt and had a connection with Jack so we had an inkling he would be there. Sure enough, he was present and saying hello, glad to be with us in this way. As I went into my own form of channel for the healing energies to flow, I noticed a huge snake wrapping its body around Adele. I was shocked and a little taken aback until I remembered that, many years earlier, Adele kept a pet snake, a large reticulated python. I quietly asked her, "What was the name of that snake you had?" She replied, "Ara. Is she here?" I smiled, "Yes, she is here with you right now." It was great validation for Adele because she often felt Ara around her, a guide of sorts. Well, she certainly was around! All of Ara's 17 feet long and 80 pounds essence was lovingly wrapping herself right around Adele's tiny body. That was my introduction to seeing spirit animals as well.

Another session with Adele was full of spirit guides and animals but one beautiful being stood out among all the rest. I saw an enormous silverback gorilla near Adele. He was so full of light and love that my awareness of this majestic being brought instant tears to my eyes. He was a powerful spirit guide for Adele and asked her to learn to communicate with him; he has information he wants her to share with others. Other animals related to her previous career as a Wildlife Rehabilitation Volunteer ended up being with her too, along with St. Francis of Assisi. This session was astounding and I was so happy to be opening doors for the spiritual realm in all of its expressions. Jack jokingly told Adele he felt like her zookeeper. He still maintains his sense of humor on the other side. Adele and I both felt light-hearted and loved.

And then it happened. I crashed emotionally and went into a tailspin. I was so confused! I had this awe-inspiring spiritual relationship with my beloved. Yet, in the moments leading to the winter holidays, all I wanted was to have Jack on the planet with me, not in spirit form but in flesh and blood, able to hold me at night, to soothe my wounded soul. So, what did I do?

I dove into the pain of heartbreak. I was alone. I found myself not feeling Jack. My family was in other places and I was utterly alone in my grief. I had friends who would have been by my side in a flash but I needed to face this alone. I cried until my eyes were swollen and I could not breathe through my nose. I developed a massive headache. I stayed in bed. I did not shower. My hair was a matted mess. I did not care. I wanted to curl up and grieve my loss. And I did. But you know what? I was okay with it. I was not worried about this dark episode. I knew it would pass, despite feeling I wanted to die and join him, while at the same time cursing him for leaving me. It was not my soul path to get lost. I had work to do with Jack, me in the physical realm, him in the spiritual. I knew that with every fiber of my being, so I allowed the emotional waves to crash.

It was a couple of weeks before I began to surface again, exhausted from my release but more robust for the experience. Grief is so different for everyone so judgment of how it is supposed to look is folly. We are unique souls with our own signature and vibration. It is most important to tap into what we each need when experiencing grief. Grief is personal, ours to know and understand in our own body. It is healthy and cleansing to own our grief, to allow the waves to crash but be careful not to let grief become who we are, to overtake our life force, our identity. Each of us survives for a reason. I survive for a reason. Jack is gone, did not survive, his leaving part of his soul contract with me. I slowly allowed myself to experience gratitude once more.

We are all much stronger than we realize and, in the face of adversity, we find courage, resolve, and HEART. When we find our hearts and step into the higher-level energies of love and compassion, we often find gratitude is there, a gentle and silent antidote to our pain. Gratitude has a way of alchemizing and shifting awareness from our individual suffering to seeing life from a bigger perspective, the one connected to Source, the divinity within connected to all.

The more I practice seeing and experiencing my world from a state of gratitude, the more peace I find. Does it mean I don't feel the intensity of loss? Absolutely not! It means that I understand I can feel it all, say yes to it all, and still find comfort in my world. Life throws us curves, the road wrought with hazards. There is no way to avoid challenges, changes, and being influenced and impacted by the world around us. The critical questions are: How resilient can we be? Can we find our grateful soul?

With a genuine sense of thankfulness, I had another session with Sherry at the end of the year, December 31. Jack came through to her, strong and clear. He wanted me to learn how to feel him more. He told me he had been beside me the entire time I was not sensing him, so, at this moment, he asked me to feel into the energy around my body. Did I feel a change in temperature? I could feel a cool sensation on my right side. The more I released my thinking mind and moved into my body, the more visceral the cool sensation became. He told me this was him. He was right next to me. It was my sign he was near, the beautiful cool sensation of his spirit. He told me to pay attention to the feeling because he is never not here.

He reminded me this is exactly what we came to do; we planned death as a part of our journey together. He said death awareness is our journey going forward. He is holding open an energetic portal between his world, the in-between world, and my world, the physical third dimension of Earth. He knows this is supporting me. He reminded me to keep letting go of my thinking brain, relax into the feeling. Feeling is energy. Trust in the energy. His job on that side is to keep the portal open so the work can continue to evolve. This is the next stage of the journey. He said all of my guides and spirit teams are waiting in the wings for me to fully embrace where this journey is going. They are holding space for me while I walk in that direction. They are waiting for me to get ready because the way this journey unfolds could help so many souls. They encouraged me to keep walking, trusting, channeling, and doing readings for people. Maybe they had to keep reminding me to trust because the thought of offering mediumship readings for people scared the hell out of me. The spirits and beings on the other side did not frighten me. I knew them. Their extraordinary light and energy were wonderful to feel when I connected with them; I felt completely protected and safe. However, my fear of people's judgments, disbeliefs, and doubts affected me the most. I needed to move past the nagging brain loop that questioned, "What would people think of me?"

I needed to know Jack was near. It soothed the wound. It had been quite the year. New Year's Eve, saying goodbye to 2019, was a milestone forever embedded into my soul. It was a year of intense growing, expanding, trusting, moving through, letting go, understanding, from pure love, a higher plan, higher purpose in what Jack and I came to do. He was remarkable here on this planet and he continues to be awe-inspiring. It hasn't stopped.

Jack's Message

Hello, my love. I'm happy we connected. Thank you. I am glad you opened the channel and set aside your judgments. Many beings, spirits, guides, light beings, angels, animal spirits, elemental beings, ascended masters, and so many more are ready and willing to meet you. The portal for communication exchange is open. I am at the gate, your assistant.

All those who read, the vastness around the human is hard for humans to fathom but each person has a team of loving, higher-dimensional beings in wait, ready to assist where and when they can. The flavor of that connection is influenced and controlled by the human. Humans are sovereign; they have control over their own essence. Free will is a beautiful part of the natural unfolding of universal expansion, expanded wisdom, and awareness. Many humans are considered lightworkers, way-showers, the advance light team, here to hold energy and keep the door open for others, shining light into the abyss of eternal life.

It can be scary for some people to recognize spirit communication (mediumship). Some may fear they are crazy or think they made up what they saw or heard. I can reassure you that, in those moments, reality is blurred. The third dimension is exposed but more illusory. People are learning to see through the density of the third dimension, to feel the higher vibrations around them, to recognize their beautiful light. I am excited to help people let go of and lessen their fear, judgment, and misunderstanding of these communications.

Your loved ones over here can offer much comfort. Let them in; acknowledge their presence even if you don't feel it right away. Let the thinking mind relax. Trust the small nudges, the whip of a breeze, the visual impressions of an image, however slight or blurred. We are ready to help you clear your energetic eyes, hone your sensory awareness, signal your ears to our frequencies.

All you need to do is keep breathing into your body. Allow the connection and trust we are there. You are never alone, always surrounded by beings of higher dimensions. Your loved ones are not held back by you making contact. They want to connect, to help you remember how to work with them, with them beside you. It is part of human evolution to bridge our realms.

My love, you provided a wonderful bridge for others this month. Keep breathing through the heartache of missing me. I am here.

January - Riding the Waves of Loss, Grief, and Joy

"You have a book to write, my love. Keep trusting."
Jack, January 12

I was coming out of the dark place when I found light, love, and acceptance. It was the beginning of a new year, and I wanted to set the stage with gratitude. My New Year's Eve session with Sherry had lifted my heart and I was feeling alive with opportunity, the spark of creativity birthing. What would my extrasensory life look like? How will it unfold? I wanted to explore these questions and more with a fresh outlook.

I invited a small group of wonderful women to come together in the studio to create vision boards, pulling together magazine images and words to help us set the tone we wanted to create in the new year. The day was led by a wonderful friend, Megan, who is skilled in assisting others in creating visions in a free-flowing, creative way. We laughed, cried, held space for each other as we glued our paper inspirations onto our boards. The day was beautifully inspiring.

I found many images symbolizing what I wanted to create and honor. Jack and our connection were a large part of my vision board, of course, but I was also clear I needed to support my life force. I am still here on this planet. I am not leaving anytime soon, as far as I know. I had no idea what all of this newfound connection with Jack and my guides would look like but that was okay. I was allowing flow to happen.

I signed up for Lee Harris's 2020 Rebirth class which helped solidify in me the forward movement I was feeling. I enlisted in Brendon Burchard's Performance Academy. I felt like I had come out of the fog, for a minute.

Then...

I had no idea the first piece of paper pulled from the Gratitude Jar I made a couple of years earlier would bring me to my knees. I read the words and felt my chest grow heavy, my heart breaking, my breath shallow and labored. Tears were welling from deep within my body. Through tear-glazed eyes, I read Jack's words, "I am grateful the most beautiful woman on the planet is sharing her life with me!" Then the breathtaking sobs took hold.

It was a strange experience. I felt the enormous swell of eternal gratitude for the love I shared with my soul mate, the love of my life, and at the same time, the heartbreak of his presence leaving the planet. His leaving was way too soon.

I had been in such a great space that day, feeling motivated, moving forward with a sense of peace in my heart. That is why I felt strong enough to read notes in the jar. Somehow it seemed an essential activity for me, with the energy of the new year pulsing, pulling me forward, and I wanted to add it to the vision board I had created a few days earlier. I had no idea the wave of grief would come crashing onto the shores of my internal landscape as hard as it did. It had been only a few days before that I had exited the sadness fog enveloping me from the holidays.

But in those moments of sobbing, I spoke to Jack, letting him know how much I loved his thinking of me that way, his loving me so deeply in the 12 years we shared. I am forever grateful for our time together. I thanked him for having a hand in this now moment, this moment of raw emotion I accepted and welcomed with open arms. I was learning to come to terms with the loss despite my extraordinary connection to Jack's soul.

During those waves of emotion, I knew I had a story to write for my publisher's upcoming book, *The Grateful Soul, The Art And Practice Of Gratitude*. Gratitude was the foundation of how I came to experience my new reality with Jack. The words flowed from my hands with ease and the writing of the journey, the work Jack and I contracted to do, was taking shape.

In mid-January, I offered a Reiki Level I and II class. This was the second class held in Jack's music studio since he passed. I kept the studio intact, not feeling the need to change or let go of any of his music gear. The studio was our vision together when we opened our business, Step Stone. There was no need to drop the forward movement in creating offerings for the public afforded by the studio. I just had to put my heart around what that might look like now, without the magic man playing music and being the background support with technology.

Step Stone music studio is a lovely space that holds an energy of sacred expansion. Most people who enter the space feel the energy, even though they may not have the words or know why it feels the way it does. A frequently repeated comment is, "Wow! This is an amazing space. It feels so good in here." Together, we created a vibrational field of higher dimensional energy. Jack and I often cleared the energy in the space, his empathic ability always signaling when clearing of the energetic field needed to take place. In other words, the studio has been a haven of higher dimensional energies for some time, intentional creativity a constant source of power. That amplified when we went through the death process together, in that amazing space full of love and spirit support. It might be hard for some people to understand but death is a sacred event during which, if done through conscious awareness, the environment takes on the air of the divine. The studio is infused with light, creating a resonance that reaches people's hearts.

There were seven Reiki students and two of us master teachers. It was a mix of males and females of different ages and backgrounds, a beautiful blend of energies. I knew three of the attendees had lost loved ones, two of them losing children in their twenties. I knew Jack would be there. Most people feel him in the space and we were working with the Reiki energies so divine healing energy was in full flame.

In meditation, I found myself on my familiar forest path with the beautiful meadow off to one side. Jack appeared on the path and we embraced, laughed, and walked arm-in-arm down it together. He said, "Follow me" and took me down the trail to our favorite beach. We walked onto the sand and spied a log washed up onshore. We sat down next to it, enjoying the moment. Then, all of a sudden, others started to show up on the beach. Jack began playing music and the mood was festive. The other spirits seemed to want to join in, playing, laughing, enjoying the ocean. My friend's husband started playing music with Jack. The young woman I had met in December was there, another friend's son, a female I did not know, and three other spirits connected to the other class members. It was a lovely scene, full of life, light, great joy. The young man started to play in the surf with the dolphins, who surrounded him. The entire group of souls on the beach were watching, laughing, in joy.

Then, above the ocean waters, I saw a figure I recognized; it was Jesus approaching from a blinding light. This moment was so beautiful it brought tears to my eyes; I felt his love and compassion. He wanted to remind us we are a family, all one, those on that side and us here on this side, separation an illusion. As the souls started to gather with him, they all walked away into the brilliant light. The only one who stayed behind was Jack. He looked at me and said, "Yes, this is part of our work, awakening others, connecting the dimensions." Then he left and I stayed on the beach, looking over the ocean, feeling complete peace.

I was a bit hesitant to share this experience out loud with the others as my thinking mind grabbed hold; I had no idea what their belief systems were or how they would react. I had had personal interactions with Jesus before this but never in a group message. I listened quietly while everyone else shared their journeys, a little uneasy about saying anything. Then I remembered something Sherry had told me, "If Spirit gives you a message for others, you have been given a gift to share. It is your job as a medium to clearly share with no judgment about how they will receive." Hearing her voice say that in my mind prompted me to share the meditation journey with the others.

I described what I had seen. I had seen a female soul on the beach connected to the woman I had just met minutes before our meditation. I told her I was not sure who the soul was but she seemed young and vibrant. The woman started crying and said, "It was my daughter. I lost her a couple of years ago. She was in her twenties." I was amazed and so grateful for Spirit gifting me the vision and for me letting the ego quiet while adding voice to the gift. Five of the seven people in that room had a beloved child or partner who passed and the other two had loved ones, perhaps not as close, but family members. We all ended up with our loved ones showing up and reminding us they are near and full of love, joy, and light.

It is up to us to remember how to connect. The veil between dimensions is thinning for all of humanity. We are evolving as a human species. People will begin to have their own synchronistic divine happenings, not to be explained but understood from within a knowing resonance in the body. More and more people will experience connection to those who have passed on, the guides who are supporting them, the energetic being of Gaia, the elemental kingdom, galactic beings. The list goes on and on but, no matter what belief system is used, human evolution and ascension are happening. We just have to learn to trust and let the thinking mind relax into the body. The body is key, the radar to multidimensional signals.

I learned to ride the waves of missing Jack's physical form and feeling bliss in the energetic connection we shared. It was a multidimensional awakening into deeper aspects of my being, affecting the way I expressed myself. It was a constant effort to remind myself it was all okay that I was experiencing this new reality some call mediumship or channeling. Many times, it felt more tangible than the third dimension (3D) world in which I found myself, and yet the fact I was still here in 3D was the other side of the equation. Our work could not happen any other way. I had to be here, he had to be there. Jack reminded me to keep playing in the magic. It is in the magic where life evolves.

Jack's Message

My love, honor your heart. Walk tenderly with your emotions. The task of loss is not easy on the human. It is much easier for me because I am home. The physical energy withdrawal you feel is real.

All those who read, when you are in human form, you have an energetic field or signature that is you, your unique flavor. When you join with your beloved, together on earth, your energy fields blend. The blending of your individual energies creates a unique dish, a new flavor, the flavor of human connection. This dish changes when your beloved leaves the planet; the flavor created together shifts. It becomes a different flavor than what you experienced prior to coming together because your unique individual flavor has been forever shifted, never going back to your original. The hint of your beloved lingers but is no longer a strong ingredient in the dish; it has become a subtle essence that can be tasted but it takes effort, a different mechanism or discernment.

People can learn how to continue to taste the flavor of their beloved. There are many ways and, because each person is unique, each will develop a way that works best for them.

You, my love, see me in meditation. You channel-write with me. I come to you in dreams; you see me in nature and even technology. You notice the small events and see the magical connection to my Spirit. Encourage others to see the magic, the joy that is the higher realms.

When people tap into joy, they are close to their beloveds, their spiritual teams, a thin veil away. We cannot force anyone to see us, feel us, connect with us. We wait for you as humans to make the decision, create the awareness. What I can share is this: we are still a part of your dish, of the beautiful human melding you created together that transformed but never fully leaves your delicious creation. The opportunity is for you to find the new flavor of your life with your beloveds love and support from this realm.

My love, thank you for writing.

February - A Loved One Goes into Hospice

"The angels are strong in your field and are supporting this work we both do.

There are so many souls who can find ease by our work, through our work.

I am happy you are stepping forward."

Jack, February 6

I continued to find ways to support my exploration into mediumship while my doubts became more subdued. With each Reiki session, each channeling encounter, my trust grew. But it seemed my acceptance was slower in coming. I felt blocked by my lack of confidence. The little girl in me who was shy and did not feel good enough for this gift of mediumship was showing herself to be recognized, hugged, and taught self-confidence. Thus, I sought mentors who could help me on this journey to understanding more about the evolution of consciousness becoming my lifeline for living in the physical without my love.

I attended a Lee Harris training in the first part of the month. I had mentored with Lee for many years and followed his work as an intuitive. He played a significant role in my personal evolution. Many of the teachings he shared became part of my training ground in allowing my natural intuitive abilities to come to the forefront. One of the practices I learned from Lee many years ago was free-flow (channel) writing. It is a powerful way to connect to spirit and receive messages. I quiet my mind and breathe into my body, becoming aware of my breath, feeling into my heart space. I calm the external mind and then I write. I ask specific questions or just remain open to any information that wants to come through. For me, it is easier to channel-write with a pen in hand than typing into a computer but this is different for everyone. The task is to write without conscious thought, just allow words to flow freely onto the page. The biggest hurdle is to trust whatever information comes through. I remind myself it is not coming from my ego-mind but another source, my connection to a higher realm. This practice has been an enormous gift for me in connecting to Jack and receiving information from my guides and loved ones.

My next session with Sherry proved to be an exercise in remembering I really do have a strong connection to Spirit; we all do if we choose to see, seek, and experience it. Sharing the information I received was part of my growth into this new way of living life, a part of the expansion into the work I was developing. I still did not know what "the work" would look like but I was learning to own who I was, step into my essence to serve others with the shield of the warrior lightworker. Jack was right by my side cheering me on.

I had the opportunity for an akashic record reading done by a sensational young woman, Emily, a gifted intuitive holistic life coach. The akashic record is a universal field of consciousness where a complete record of past events is held, as a living, energetic library. Many people cn see into the living library to read someone's records, their soul path blueprint, and archetypes related to their soul's desired expression in this life. This reading was exceptional; numerous Aha moments brought even more solidity to the reasons certain aspects of my journey were unfolding the way they were, layers of an onion continuing to fall away and my soul blueprint shining brighter.

We started with breathwork. I cannot reiterate strongly enough how important being aware of the breath is to arriving into the body and tapping into intuition. How does the breath feel? Does it feel better on the inhale or on the exhale? I was creating body awareness as I moved into my mind's intuitive eyes. I went into my sacred soul spot, a vast crystal cave.

Jack was there, along with my guide Kishma. Jack was so excited I was there with him. We wound our way along the path around the outside edge of the crystal cave, massive pillars of brilliant crystal formations emanating an energetic pulse. The cave was luminous and bright multi-colored light was glowing from within the stones. When we arrived at the bottom of the cave, there was a small lake. At the lake's edge was a sandy beach but this beach was not of stone; the sand was tiny, clear crystals in all the light spectrum colors, glistening from reflected lights in the cave. Jack and I sat down on the beach, looked out over the water, and relaxed into the sand. My guide Kishma was standing near. As I slowly came back from this sacred spot, the akashic reading began.

Emily was surprised to notice I had a lot of life force vitality; she felt I was being supported by Jack's luminosity, the energetic tie he held for me and our continued work. While part of me was questioning why Jack had to leave so we could do this work together, another part understood and was ready. I was being called to rise into the role of teacher, facilitator, medicine woman, and innovator. My guides told Emily I wanted to make an impact in life, to leave a legacy to help others. My guides said I care deeply about shifting something in the world in a big way. The question became: could I tap into the legacy I wanted to leave in the world?

Immediately, I shared the answer to that question with Emily. The words poured out of my mouth, fast and furious before I had a chance to analyze or second guess them. I knew conscious death was what I wanted to share, the knowledge our life is not done when we leave this planet, that as a soul we are just a thin veil away, ready to engage when appropriate. We are so much more than we have been led to believe. I want to help people remember who they are, remember we are all on track, following (loosely perhaps) a blueprint we created before we incarnated into human form. We can tap into the sacred, eternal side of ourselves. Our loved ones on the other side are close, ready to connect and support this awareness. I want to facilitate people awakening to their multidimensional self.

Wow! I could feel Jack jump for joy at that moment as I realized the task I was being pulled toward, mapping out the journey, creating my journey, and leading others on their journey. I was still not sure how this looked but it was clear that Jack was facilitating from the other side, both of us working in tandem, plugged into source energy. It could be called a mainline connection to the divine. Emily called it a hotline to God.

Who knew I would have another opportunity to fully tap into that mainline connection to Source with another loved one going into the death process? My landlord, Jay, my adopted father, went into hospice care. On learning of Jack's impending death, he was the one who cried, "It should be me, not you! I have lived a long, good life; you are so young with so much to live for. It should be me!"

Jack had been concerned his death would be hard on Jay's health, as he had become increasingly frail over the last year. Jack's leaving did hit him hard and, while he was a trooper in his final months, his health went quickly downhill.

I had been giving Jay Reiki a couple of times a week since January to help with pain and discomfort. When he headed into ER toward the end of February, none of us thought he would return home. I visited him and his wife Donna in hospice and was grateful I could be with them for a little while, unsure how much longer he would live.

I had planned a trip a year earlier with my mom and, while I hesitated to leave, Jack reassured me he would be with Jay. He said, "Do not worry, as you know, I will be there to greet him when he passes. His body is slow to leave. It is all okay and on track. He will be greeted by many. Donna will need your support and love. Give freely to her." So, I kissed Jay on the forehead and told him I loved him and would see him when I returned. Walking out the door knowing it could be the last time we speak, at least in this way, was difficult for me.

The trip with Mom was a fun and enlivening adventure and my spirits lifted as we enjoyed our time together, mother and daughter, two widows who shared the journey of love, loss, and life after losing a loved one. We both needed to soothe our souls with laughter and time together. Mom had been my foundation when I needed it the most, during the last days of Jack's death walk. We now shared a similar discovery into what would evolve in our lives without our beloveds with us in physical form. This discovery was not planned or wanted but required.

Jack's Message

Hello, my love. It is so nice to hear you laugh, to see you smile, to be with you in the discovery of joy. You are learning to be more comfortable with our new relationship and I am elated. Do you feel that?

All who read, I am pleased to share that, at this point in experiencing our book, you will have had nudges from your beloveds, your light family, the angelic realm. The legions of beings from higher dimensions are working with us, in your Now, walking through the pages with you. The numbers are more than you can comprehend. We are offering an opportunity for moments of awakening to your unique connection with spirit. We are cheering you on. Remember, remember, remember what you forgot when you came into physical form!

This is the time you chose to incarnate (bring your light being into human form) on the planet. This is the life you chose in which to experience Earth's ascension. This is the moment you chose to be. Can you feel it?

Breathe into me for a moment. I want all of you to experience part of what Becki and I do together. Take a nice deep breath into your heart and breathe into your body. Part of my task from my realm of existence is to help you feel into tapping in and working with higher dimensional energies. This was not something Becki was expecting, so I am glad she is able to allow the flow of words and set her thinking mind aside.

If you choose, you can do this activity with me. Take a few minutes, put the book down and breathe into the awareness of your loved ones here. I am your gatekeeper; you need not fear. We are working with higher-dimensional, divine energy. You are safe. Again, breathe into your heart, breathe into your loved ones; they are near. Do not doubt. Trust in this moment. They are already with you; close your eyes, drop into your heart, breathe, and ask them to connect. Then let go of any expectation and wait for a response. Notice colors or pictures in your third eye (your imagination), sensations in your body, emotions, words that pop into your mind, unexpected sounds. Avoid analyzing or questioning these experiences. Simply notice.

Becki saw the following in a meditation although she did not realize what she was seeing at the time. Now she knows. The light from each of your hearts is connecting to each other across the Earth plane, creating a massive web of light. The light from all of you then connects to all your beloveds in Spirit, your family of light, blending into a solid, pulsing, brilliant light, connecting the Earth plane to the Cosmos. Feel into the immeasurable power of this dancing, radiating light. We are co-creating a new fifth-dimensional Earth.

Thank you for playing with me.

Thank you, my love, for going with what was coming through, allowing the words to flow.

March - Others on the Death Journey

"Conscious death is what we did, my love, our path together.
Who better than you to share this journey with others?"
Jack, April 22

When I arrived back from my trip, Jay was home. He had
had a rough couple of days but his health had improved
enough for him to leave hospice at the hospital. What a relief
to be able to be with them in this challenging time of letting
go! I knew I would be able to participate in his walk toward
the death passage with many of the tools I had learned
through Jack's death walk. I was also able to use what I was
learning from Jack's spirit and implemented some of the new
techniques with Jay. This was part of our work together. My
heart was still raw from the loss just six short months earlier
but I could not deny the presence of the death passage in my
life again.

I knew I had the ability to hold space for Jay and Donna: to
be in the room with them, walking the journey, listening to
what they felt to share, holding their hands when needed,
watching the process unfold while standing in compassion,
carrying the energetic frequency of light for both of them. I
had been through this with my beloved; I could certainly do
it with another person I deeply loved. It seemed natural. I
was working in two worlds: the third dimension of the

physical and the in-between space where Jack and I meet. It is a gift to be shared.

Jay was able to be under at-home hospice care. As long as Donna and I could take care of his needs with the traveling nurses' support, he was comfortable at home. He was clear of mind and able to converse, watch TV, and interact with us. His body was in the slow process of shutting down. Toward the end of the month, I was going upstairs twice a day to offer him energy healing. It seemed Reiki was the one thing that calmed him enough to be able to sleep at night. I also began using sandalwood, frankincense, myrrh, and cedarwood sacred oils. Every time I offered healing, I rubbed his swollen feet with those oils blended in a carrier oil, lovingly reassuring him he was doing a great job.

At one point during a session, while in my meditative state, I saw a beautiful angelic-like woman standing next to him. She looked at him with complete love and informed me she was his grandmother. She told me she was grateful to me for caring for her lineage. It was noticed. When I came out of the session, I thought it strange she used the word lineage but, when I shared the information with Jay and Donna, it made perfect sense to them. Jay was 91 years old, his grandmother from a time when that language was used. In their religious belief, the ancestry line is crucial and she was there for her lineage, her grandson. She told me she would be present when he crossed over. Jay was touchingly grateful. He had asked me with genuine concern if anyone would be there to meet him when he passed. Now he knew at least two souls, Jack and Jay's grandmother would greet him with open arms. It helped ease his worry. Jay rested into his process.

One night I invited Donna to join us in the room during our healing session. Jay fell asleep and, when I sensed the healing energy flow was finished, I went over to the small couch and sat next to Donna. I held her hand and we listened in silence as we watched him breathe. We both just watched his breath, in and out. He had been struggling to breathe, just like Jack. I was quietly sending Donna healing energy and, after about 20 minutes she said to me, "You are giving me Reiki too, aren't you? I can feel it." I smiled and whispered, "Yes." We continued watching Jay sleep, our silence an honoring of his life force. I sent love to Donna, this beautiful woman who had been married to Jay for over 70 years. There are no words to describe the moment other than to say a sacred energy filled the room. We both loved this man who was soon to be leaving. I felt immense gratitude for Jack and what we shared. I knew it was helping me at this moment to hold a safe container for Donna, as I knew the task ahead would be life-altering for her in a way only experienced by living it.

In between giving Reiki sessions to Jay, I saw other clients and found synchronicity playing a big role in my forward movement. I started meeting more people whose lost loved ones had come back to them from the spiritual realm. I found clients ready and willing to work with their guides, open to what happened in their Reiki sessions. It seemed the work

Jack and I had agreed to do was taking form but none of this would have happened if people were not ready and open to seeing with a broader, more expansive vision.

In free-flow writing, I asked Jack how I could keep our lines of communication open to best serve others and he said, "Just do it, Becki. Keep asking and trusting I am here. I am never going anywhere. It is up to you to decide how, when, and where, but know I am near and will always be. Ground into your own beingness. Breathe into the awareness this is who you are. You have always carried the light powerfully. I love you so much for that, as you helped me balance while there with you. You have to keep letting the thinking mind relax. You are doing this. It is me more than you realize."

My story was not unique. The fact I was meeting others who had contact with their deceased loved ones made me realize afterlife communication can occur with anyone, if the person still here is open to that connection. It is more common than any of us realize. I witnessed this as people started coming out of the woodwork to share their own magical experiences. The communication varied but the common theme was the energy of love never ending.

I began mentoring Kris, a client who wanted to make conscious contact with her daughter, Liberty. Jack had been strongly present in sessions with her and he seemed to have a special relationship with Liberty on the other side. Kris wanted me to ask Jack if he had any insight into how to help her connect. When I asked him, he responded, "Address her blocks about not being able to see and hear first. Then do an exercise of breathing into your bodies, grounding into the body. Lie down if that helps. Visualize bright white light raining down on you. Bathe in that light, inhale that light, allow it to fill you. Then invite us both into your energy field. I can help. Liberty is ready to work with her, to communicate in this way. Ask her to feel around her body. Where does she want to feel Liberty? Liberty will help her. Tell her to keep feeling into that same place; it will become familiar to her. She will know what Liberty being near feels like, just like you feel me now. Start her with free-flow, channel writing to see how that goes. Have her release judgments, allow flow without mind." We started by using Jack's suggestions and Kris soon felt Liberty near her. It was the beginning of a new, expanded relationship for them in a positive and uplifting way that continues to flourish and grow.

The reality of my connection to Jack became even more evident. Sharing the death journey was evolving into becoming part of my passionate, afterlife connection work.

I met a remarkable woman named Eartha through a friend of hers with whom I was acquainted in an online group. Toward the end of the month, Eartha and I met on a Zoom conference call, the most convenient method for us as she is from England. She had lost her partner Steve suddenly through an accident, leaving him in a coma for three days before he passed. The reason I made contact was that Steve had come quickly to Eartha after he left the body and I felt she could use support from someone who had the same afterlife connection with their beloved. Jack was nudging me to connect and, once on the call, we both knew this was destined.

Steve had been sharing information with Eartha that was so similar to what Jack shared with me; we felt we were all connected. In fact, Steve and Jack knew each other and both said we are part of a soul group family, our working together similar and complementary. It was a relief we found each other, women on the path of navigating the 3D world without their partners, yet experiencing a profound spiritual connection to their souls.

Amidst all of the synchronicity, I found my attention focused on Jay. He was in the depths of transition and I did not want to miss this profound opportunity to support him along the way. I felt Jack was always near, ready to help from his realm.

Jack's Message

> *The stage is being set, my love. Conscious death is a passage you are walking through again. I am always near, holding you, beside you, breathing with you as you intuit how to respond to the moments of life as they arise.*

All who read, as humanity rises in consciousness, into higher states of awareness, the creation of an en-light-ened death process will emerge, or let me say, remembered. Throughout Earth's time, people have known how to honor death. But, for thousands of years, they have been veiled from the truth of their light, the truth of their beingness, the truth of their journey.

So many souls are in a type of contract to assist Earth into a higher frequency, the fifth-dimension, and are incarnating onto the Earth plane. As we move closer, the veils thin, dimensions meld, and people begin to remember who they are: spirit in human form. The third-dimension is a wonderful matrix. I loved so much of my life there; you my love, our touch, nature, music. But it is dense; being sensitive, I struggled with that aspect.

Density is shifting, the veil thinning. Loved ones in this realm are eager, ready, sending love for support at this time of great upheaval. Huge change is reality and the more people wake up, remember they are a light being in form, the easier it will be to start accessing the available higher frequencies. They will be closer to Spirit and will be able to communicate and collaborate in a whole new, divine way.

We need those who are on the planet showing the way. Death is only a transformation back into whom we are, a homecoming. It is not easy while in body form. You are honored beyond measure by Spirit, your loved ones, your family of light. You are warriors in the dense form of awakening. You are seen and loved. So many souls are right by your side, holding you. When people no longer fear death but are able to honor the passage in full awareness, humanity will take a quantum leap forward into the fifth dimension. Conscious death will be more common.

My love, hold my hand and walk with me through this awareness. When you walk with me, I can help uplift you energetically, replenish your soul. We are in this new way of relationship together, leading the way for others. You are deeply loved by Spirit. Thank you.

April - **The Last Breath**

"The vision I shared is a fifth-dimensional technology that can help others in a conscious death transition. It helps with thinning the veil between dimensions."

Jack, March 8

April was to be another intense month. I took an online Reiki training course and experienced a meditation that was a precursor in support for me to handle what was to follow.

As I drifted into meditation, I found myself walking toward a river. Jack joined me there and, as always, there was great joy in seeing each other in this field of energy vibration. The forest was full of elemental life: fairies, gnomes, and forest spirits. At the river, we both entered the water. Light began pouring into my body while Jack poured water over me. I was drinking in the healing waters, absorbing all of it into my physical form. He and I dove into the river and swam to an underground river. We laughed and frolicked and then came out of the water into an immense cavern. Thousands of souls were there. I was told these were souls who were crossing over. In addition, fifth-dimensional beings were present, all cheering the work Jack and I are here to do. I also saw Steve, smiling in acknowledgment of many souls together on this path of transition awareness. Suddenly I was traveling; I felt myself standing on a mountaintop overlooking a beautiful landscape of snow-covered peaks with a legion of angels honoring the Earth. Then, I was in space looking back on Earth, the living Gaia was a sentient, breathing being, radiant with all the crystals of the lands shining out. I came back to the land, feeling her breathe, knowing all is well with the journey ahead.

A couple of months before Jack passed, we had a conversation about something he had seen. This happened before the coughing started, close to the time he began to get sick. He was sitting in the studio, directly facing a friend across the coffee table. They were chatting about the day, mostly work challenges. The conversation was steeped in the 3D matrix, ordinary, not metaphysical. Suddenly, in the empty chair next to his friend, Jack saw an image that caused him to blink several times; he was having an otherworldly vision while the conversation rolled on. Jack had a hard time focusing on his friend's words as the image became front and center in his awareness.

A circular ring of beautiful crystals was slowly spinning clockwise. The center was open, allowing a clear view of the chair behind. The ring was about one foot in diameter and the crystals were small, standing out about an inch from the edge, clustered around each other, shimmering with light. The colors were radiant, the full spectrum of the rainbow and more. This object was suspended in the air as it rotated. Jack was in awe of what he was seeing. *What is this vision,* he thought to himself? Then the ring of crystals moved through the air toward him. As it came closer, it grew in size, brilliant in its slow spin. After a couple of minutes, the ring slowly retreated back to the chair, resuming the original position. Finally, it dissipated from his view. Though perplexed, he did not mention what had just occurred to his friend, but he couldn't wait until I got home to share.

We had no idea what this image meant. We knew it was a higher dimensional communication and speculating about it was fun. Jack felt it was from his guides. We played around with what it could signal for him but eventually moved onto other matters, not having any intuitive hits on his astounding vision. Shortly after that, Jack got sick and the focus shifted. I did not think about it again until, one night during the first part of April, the vision Jack described came pushing into my awareness. It was so strong I felt it was important to learn what this message meant.

I asked Jack if he could help me understand why the image came into my field of vision so powerfully. He told me it is a fifth dimensional (5D) energy technology, a dimensional key used for specific purposes to help meld the dimensional fields, creating a sort of collapse. In other words, it thins the veil. Jack said his guides were helping him because he needed the veil to be thinner in order to perform conscious death. He told me I had used this crystal ring technology before, in another time, another life. He implored me to remember, saying it can help others.

Once again, I was learning to step into trust and to honor my intuitive abilities. Right away, I started to use this beautiful ring of crystals while in Reiki sessions with Jay. He had beseechingly asked me, "How long is this going to last? I am ready to go. Why am I not going? Jack was able to go so quickly." He invited me to help him so, when this 5D information came in from Jack, I felt guided to use it in meditation while working with Jay.

At this time, I was connecting with Jack regularly; I needed his support as these experiences with Jay were intensifying my own feelings of pain and loss. There were times when I was giving Jay Reiki that I flashed on giving Jack Reiki, almost as if the timeline was jumping around and I was touching my beloved. Jack reminded me to move the energy through my body, saying, "Do not doubt the guidance you are receiving. It is your doubt that trips up the energy and causes it to get hung up, so keep moving it through and out of your body."

He told me he was with Jay a lot now, as Jay was moving into the in-between. Jack verified my experiences by saying, "You did see his celestial family; many are around him, Donna, and his children right now. I don't know all of them but we will all be here when his soul decides it is time to let go fully."

I used the crystal ring vision as part of my nightly routine for Jay. I would engage the Reiki healing energy and rub his feet with whatever sacred oil I was guided to use. I offered love as I anointed his feet, a holy act of compassion and honor. I felt that pure energy flowing from my heart to Jay's. Then at some point, I would feel Jack or Jay's grandmother and visualize the crystal ring. I was amazed to find the ring slowly spun above Jay and then, ever so gradually, started to move from vertical to horizontal orientation and rest into his heart. His whole body lit up from the sparkling crystals.

When I was with Jay the night before Easter, he seemed distressed, as though something had shifted. He was afraid. I looked him in the eyes and reminded him he knew how to do this, that it was okay; he was surrounded by loved ones both here and there. He relaxed into receiving healing frequencies. I knew his passage was near; I saw a stunning angelic being hovering over him. Jay was grateful for the reassurance.

The next day, Easter Sunday, I received a panicked call from Donna; Jay was having seizures. She and their son were doing what they could to help him while waiting for the hospice nurse. I ran upstairs to be with all of them. It was not easy; Jay was in a challenging place of body shut-down. I stood at his feet, holding him, sending encouragement. As I looked into his eyes, I saw what I had seen in Jack's eyes just before he passed, the look of life in transition, the eyes signaling the letting go of the body. The hospice nurse said to Donna, "Go to his side. He is getting ready to leave."

Donna was caressing him, their son and me in prayer. Donna looked across the bed, thinking someone was standing near, but she did not see anyone. Then she felt Jack behind her. He was so strong she expected to see him. When Jay fell silent, Donna said she felt a rush of energy move through her body. She believed Jay had moved through her to go to Jack and the others there to greet him. It was a beautiful, sacred, yet heartbreaking moment. I was elated for Jay who finally made his way home and saddened by our loss of him here in physical form.

I stayed with Jay until they came for his body, honoring his form for as long as he was present. It was the least I could do; I loved this man who had been so much more than a landlord to Jack and me, more like a father. Strange how time warps in moments like this. In the blink of an eye, you witness eternity, the expansion of the spirit. When his body left the apartment, I felt the emptiness in his form, the separation of the energetic tie to the physical body tangible. I had felt the same emptiness when they wheeled Jack's body out the door. I will never forget the shift in the energy field. I was in awe of how much we are entwined with each other while here on the planet, in our dense physical bodies, and yet we are never disconnected from soul essence. I was glad to know I am never disconnected from Jack's soul because the next couple of weeks were not easy.

After Jay passed, I went into automatic pilot phase again, not feeling my connection with Jack much, going back to work at a part-time job, seeing clients. I was allowing myself time to dive back into my everyday work life. I was not channel writing but I did stay connected to Sherry and Eartha.

Despite my connections, I began to doubt myself again, wondering why I was struggling so much at times and then not so much at other times. I found myself on the human-experience rollercoaster. What was I continuing to seek?

But then it happened. Jack came through loud and clear. I picked up a pen and paper to write.

He reminded me life unfolds in perfect timing. Since Jay had passed, I did not feel as connected to Jack but what I did not realize was my ease in our communications felt like a conversation, no hardship, simple, no task, just flow. He told me to have a conversation with him just like what I was doing now in free-flow writing. "See how easy it is to flow, with our thoughts becoming one expression as you put the words on paper. See how we are in one thought? That is the power of your ability. You think it is just you but I am here, blending with you, in the field of awareness with you. There is no separation in this experience we now have together. What you seek is your own heart. It is the key for which you keep searching and you do not need to look further, unless you choose to do so. Your own heart is the answer you keep seeking. Write, my love, write. Your heart is a gift in your expression. You so easily tap into me this way, as if it is my hand with yours, writing the words as you feverishly get them on the page. See my hand on yours as you write, because that is what takes place. Our separate beings become one movement, one dance, as flow happens. Our love is now a part of your sharing, a part of the evolution, a part of who you and I are now. What a beautiful thing this is! We are learning to navigate multidimensional communication. You are not separate and apart from me but a melding of our souls: soul partners, many lives together, much to share with the world. You, my love, are the conduit." What felt like a disconnect was actually an ease of conversation that seemed way too simple. It couldn't be that simple, could it? Jack confirmed it was so. He was always doing his best to show me.

At the end of the month, my friend Adele and I spent a day together. I had started the week off with a migraine and was feeling slightly overwhelmed so she picked me up and took me on a drive. We journeyed to the RedSun Labyrinth to walk in the crisp, beautiful spring air. It felt good to breathe fresh air in this magical setting. The morning before the drive, I had a channel writing session with Jack and one of the things he shared with me was to breathe into him. He told me I know how to do this, our energetic tie strong. He said he could help lift me up if I just breathe into him, close my eyes and breathe him in. "Breathe into me, my love. I can help you from that space." As Adele and I were walking up the path to the labyrinth, there was a new little sculpture of a leaf on which was written, "Breathe my love. All is well." I cried as I knew he helped orchestrate our being there. Jack had loved to walk the labyrinth.

At the center of the labyrinth is an honoring altar with several divisions around the circle's outside edge, the center of the circle symbolizing divinity, god. People leave gifts and small offerings in the different divisions, or realms, labeled mineral, earth, plant, animal, human, and angelic. As I said prayers of honoring to each of the realms I was feeling into Jack.

When Jack and I went to the labyrinth, we always took crystals or agates to leave as offerings. The agates we left were a particular ocean agate found on southern Oregon beaches. I know these stones well. The offerings are frequently changed and moved around by the property owners because so many people come and leave small items. I have always had a strong tie to the angelic realm. As I studied the offerings in each section, marveling at what people leave, I noticed some small crystals like those we often left. The second my eyes landed on the angelic realm section, I was amazed to see one of our agates sitting right on top of the pile. There was no doubt the agate was one Jack had left, and in the angelic realm, my strongest higher dimensional support outside of divine source. I was in awe of the magic of the day. Jack was reminding me to notice the small, special moments. He was near, showing me.

Jack's Message

My love, how intense the human journey! I know how hard this is for you, not having me physically there. I hold deep compassion for you.

179

All who read, so many souls assist in the passage of the human form into Spirit. It is easier on the human if the spirit is free from earthly cares and burdens, but if not, there are angelic beings here who nurture and care for souls who need assistance.

Death is a passage, a walk through dimensions, that can be confusing. Some souls lose track or seem to find they don't meet their welcome-home team. If there is a sudden death or the person has unresolved trauma, the soul can be in a state of limbo. This is why it is so important to do the death awareness work, to help those who are embarking on the journey.

The closer the dimensions get, the easier it will be for souls to find their way, but for now, many are here in spirit and on the Earth plane to assist their passage. There is going to be a huge exodus of souls from the planet. The more humanity awakens to the eternal life force within the; the more fear will dissipate, the easier the passage.

Thank you to all the people who walk the earth's journey in the Now. It is a heroic journey. Thank you to the people who walk with death, understanding it is a sacred passage and honoring that passage as an act of divinity.

My love, thank you for continuing to step forward, write our book, to love despite the heartache. I am with you.

May - The Abler Soul

"I am your other half, part of the one same soul."
Jack, May 17

It is entirely natural to move in and out of states of grief and sadness followed by joy and elation with a higher conscious awareness that we are all connected in this life and beyond. I was no exception. It was like surfing an ocean wave with highs and lows, riding the crest of the wave, moving into the center surrounded by a surreal world only to find my emotions crashing onto shores of my heart. I learned to be okay with whatever I was feeling, allowing my high and low emotions to move through me, my fear and doubt to arise, be seen, and then alchemize while carrying my vulnerability on my sleeve. And write. This book, our book, was beginning to take on form and I continued to experience mediumship in my own way, my own flavor, the secret sauce that is Becki. The great thing about this human journey is we all have a secret formula unique to who we are here to be. We get to choose how we share that formula.

I read the book *The Afterlife of Billy Fingers* by Annie Kagan, an account of a woman in contact with her brother after he passed. Billy shares aspects of his life and insight into his afterlife with his sister. It was validation for me as the new path in channeling Jack continued to unfold.

My work with Sherry expanded into a beautiful realm of communication with Jack and both our guide networks while bringing the information into the tangible, using art to express what we saw in vision. The idea we were holding higher dimensional concepts and bringing them into art was a new exploration in our time together, but this process occurs when artists go to the place of no time; the creation unfolds organically, without conscious thought. We created a new form of healing together, combining meditation, vision, channeling, and art to express the magic being shown by Spirit. It was all magical.

I continued to play a part in the afterlife connection journey with Eartha as she too was staying in contact with her beloved Steve. A friend of hers recommended the book *Love is Stronger Than Death: The Mystical Union of Two Souls* by Cynthia Bourgeault. It illustrates a similar experience, describing what the journey looked like from a Christian perspective. I was happy to read anything similar to my own happenings. In her accounting, Cynthia explores the idea of a deep and undying love connection between two souls that remains strong after one part of the whole leaves the Earth plane. The mystical union continues.

Father Aidan expressed another take on the idea of the Abler Soul in his *Catacomb Catechumen blog post, Saturday, August 3, 2013*, "a Christian perspective on sexuality (the Abler Soul)"

-excerpts and thoughts from "Love is Stronger Than Death: The Mystical Union of Two Souls" by Rev. Cynthia Bourgeault

Within Christian tradition there is a class of relationships sometimes called the "Lover and the Beloved" (Song of Solomon) or the "Abler Soul" (a term from John Donne)- a particularly intense relationship that "is a path of true love" that is more than mere romance or passion "but rather...conforms to and reveals the authentic pattern of each partner's soul... the Abler Soul must be forged..."

PRECONDITIONS:

1. a strong erotic connection...

2. strong spiritual yearning...

3. innate emotional trust...

"...the Abler Souls must always be beloveds..." (because)... "the erotic, sexual energy is the specific energy through which this union of souls comes about. Sexual Energy provides the force of fusion that holds the two formerly separate individualities in the ...bonding of one soul."

"...sexual energy is understood as something very different from libido, or lust...it is the highest form of Transformational Energy, the finest and most subtle spiritual energy that human beings can work with directly... Sexual Energy is the agent of all

transformation-not just physical procreation, but Every Form of Creativity: (prayer, poetry, and spiritual transformation)... "

What was becoming clear to me is the extraordinary bond Jack and I have now is not uncommon. Many have and do experience this type of connection after one partner leaves the planet. The growth of each soul in the partnership continues to evolve. Jack and I did experience the preconditions mentioned, although we had no idea while in life together here that this was the type of relationship we had. We just knew it was intense, unique, wrapped in a love neither of us had experienced until we came together. The instant our eyes met, we knew something was pulling us forward. We felt the contract we chose to fulfill was steeped in divine love and soul evolution, a force beyond our 3D consciousness.

Was our time together all easy and flowing? No way! We challenged each other to grow, to expand, to look at and assess our paradigms and belief systems. The type of commitment it takes to evolve in a partnership that way is challenging and wrought with vulnerable exposure to the soul's deepest parts. Jack was a master at being open and vulnerable to his dark side, his less than favorable attributes, which also pushed me to see mine. We often commented that we were holding up a mirror for each other to gaze into, our souls' growth leading the way.

The more I conversed with Jack, the more I eased into an awareness of the Abler Soul, one soul essence. He had told me about this concept before I had the words to describe what Cynthia so eloquently explained in her book. Jack was ahead of me, pulling me forward. He reminded me I needed to build my energetic capacity to step fully into the task ahead, writing about our conscious death process and afterlife connection. I was gaining ground but in my own time, in my own way. He always reminded me to go easy on myself. What I faced and moving forward afterward takes great courage and he knew I also experienced excruciating heartache. "All in good time, my love," he said. "It is all okay, part of the growing and moving through my leaving."

When I step back and lean into the reality of the Abler Soul, I recognize this kind of love is the greatest love one can experience and that one partner must leave the physical plane to create the necessary expansion into the dimension of the divine. The ultimate sacrifice of undying love - love exposed wholly and without reserve, brevity on the physical plane - is often part of the equation. The reality, there is no death of love but an energy transcending both souls, with the creation of a third energy, the reality of love itself.

In an essay on Love from his book *God Is with Us*, Ladislaus Boros says: "When two people say 'we' because love has made them 'we,' in reality a new existence is created. The whole world takes on a new dimension, a new depth. This new sphere of existence is not simply 'already there;' it comes into existence as a function of the free self-giving of one person to another."

My landlord, Donna, is a woman who was blessed to have found her love early in life. They were able to spend over 70 years married on this Earth plane but have an everlasting bond, an eternal commitment. She shared a poem she wrote about her beloved, Jay. She shared that she did not know how she wrote it, the words coming to her fast and without thought. The words are poignant and beautiful, a testament to love shared by two beautiful souls who came for a long life together. It is a blessing she allowed me to share this poem with you. This too, is a great love beyond dimensions.

The Joy of Sadness
By Donna Curtis

You are gone and my heart swells
As tears overflow my eyes
So sad am I that every beat of heart
Within me cries.

I wonder will this ever leave me,
This sadness my heart bears
Then with my wonder comes a joy
That overwhelms my cares.

For with each tear and fervent plea
To Him you're with above
Comes a deepening of feeling for you both,
A deepening of love.

And, I remember how that feeling came
So many times before
When we'd agree, or even disagree,
I'd love you all the more.

For you are me, and I am you,
So many years as one
And sadness only brings to mind
That bond and then joy comes.

So, I'll be sad and welcome it
Through all my rest of years
'Cause sadness really is my joy
Of you, shown in my tears.

The idea of an Abler Soul made sense to me and I grew in my understanding of the nature of this type of love. I saw it in Donna, felt it in me. It was why the energetic tie was still so strong I literally felt Jack near, felt his touch, felt our intimacy, could hear his words, see him with my etheric eyes. Cynthia Bougeault discusses this idea in her book *The Meaning of Mary Magdalene - Discovering the Woman at the Heart of Christianity*. In her book, an anonymous mystic writes: "True love demands sacrifice because true love is a transforming force and is really the birth-pangs of union on a higher plane."

I had been experiencing those birth pangs for several months, all the while seeing the beautiful new life force birthed with Jack's death, our afterlife bond.

Jack's Message

Hello, my love. Thank you for walking this path with me, remembering who we are. As life moves forward, synchronicity will play a big role in the people you meet, those with whom you will work, learn, grow, and love. In time, you will find another human love but our love is beyond dimensions, a oneness of being that is eternal. You are growing more comfortable with that, aren't you?

All who read, I want to help people understand the death passage does not mean the end of love or soul connection. Your beloveds are not gone from you. Yes, the physical body may no longer be on the

189

planet, but their soul essence lives on, ready to commune. The transition of form does not mean finality. People can learn to feel their loved ones, sense them, communicate with them, be comforted by them. Comfort can show up in many ways, such as when you, my love, found the stone I left for you at the labyrinth. I am so glad you noticed.

There is so much fear in the world but it is showing up for humanity to see and shift, change, transmute. Some couples, those Abler Souls mentioned, have incarnated together, their connection forming a bridge between realms. Many parents and children have a strong soul connection unbroken by loss, the connection spanning dimensions.

People have forgotten they are more than the human form, the third-dimensional density keeping fear in place. When people step into the light of awareness and fear subsides, they find magic, synchronicity, life everlasting in all its many expressions: birth, life, death, spirit, all just phases of the one immortal soul.

Honor the divinity within. You have forgotten how powerful you are as humans. The ascension of Earth does not happen without you, and you are pulling the dense consciousness into higher states of frequency.

My love, thank you for honoring our two souls, our one love, and our one evolving consciousness of light.

June - The Contract with My Beloved

"Keep using your breath. Breathe into my freedom of Spirit, my Now existence. We share this wisdom journey together. We knew this at some level, our contract. Thank you for writing about it. I am full of love and gratitude for your gift of honoring our life."

Jack, June 7

I decided to dive into exploring more details of our contract. What does it mean to have a contract with another soul? Some believe, before we arrive on Earth in a physical body, each individual sets up scenarios for soul growth, orchestrating people, places, and things to help us achieve our soul's purpose this time around. We choose where we want to incarnate, the parents who would serve us best in growth, the general situations leading us to find our way. Sometimes, seemingly negative events and situations lead us to our greatest internal discoveries. From the place of Spirit, growth can be wrought with hardship only to reveal the prize of awareness, the golden ticket. In Jack's case, his parents had a direct catalytic effect on his popping in and out of dimensional fields, leading him into his life-long spiritual seeking.

The wild card is we, as humans on this planet, have free will. In other words, we can veer off the path into entirely different territory, our soul in the background gently trying to remind us, get us back on track. The routes to a desired soul purpose are vast, many roads leading to a similar outcome. The reality is that it is all okay. No matter what, we are growing, expanding, and evolving, regardless of whether we are aware of it, whether we remember our contracts. That is the beauty of ascension into higher realms. We have passed the marker, a point in human history when we are no longer going to destroy ourselves. The high vibrational light entering the planet and our human bodies signal our global ascension is guaranteed. The third, fourth, and fifth dimensional fields are moving closer together, the veils between each thinning, and soul remembrance be-coming stronger.

Jack and I played in that field of energy long before he passed. The magical field of Spirit was the very foundation of our life together. So, while it may have been a natural progression for us to perform conscious death when we knew Jack was leaving, that piece of the contract did not come into our awareness until we faced the inevitability of his soul passage. In channel Jack said, "You understand at a deeper level that my death was planned, and we agreed to do it together because it is part of your medicine in working with people now. There was really no other way for us to make this journey, to fulfill our contract. The sadness is a moment in time, a temporary state, because your true nature is love and joy."

But, occasionally, I have doubted myself, been hard on myself for not always feeling him, questioning my connection, wanting to feel him stronger, missing him. Once, in free-flow writing, I was whining to him, "But you feel distant from me, harder for me to..." Jack said, "STOP! That is your mind running in circles. You did feel me, we have intimacy. Remember that! You can and do connect with me naturally, easily. Stop doubt and self-sabotage! You and I are connected through a direct and divine channel." Even in our new relationship, we challenge each other's growth; although I have to say, it is now more one-sided with me still residing in the 3D density of human form than on Jack's side in the unbelievable freedom and love where he is. "Okay, just breathe, Becki, just breathe into your heart, just breathe into me! Your heart is the key," I hear his words echoing in my mind as I take up pen and write some more.

When Jack and I met, we knew our meeting was right on track, both of us immediately felt a strong soul connection. We thought of ourselves as soul mates. We also had memories of other lives together, other times and places. We enjoyed delving into what we felt to be true about those previous connections, other past lives when we were partners, family, or friends. I was fascinated by the awareness that our other lives seemed to be short-lived, too, with one or both of us dying early, the relationship shortened. Past life connection is a subject Eartha and I continue to explore, the idea our soul group may be highly accomplished with the death process, the passage from one form into another. Steve and Eartha have also shared many lives, this short time and passage a common theme for them as well.

I continued to be curious about Jack's Now expression so I asked him what it was like where he is and more about our contract. He said, "I am in more than one place, many places at once. I am with my family of light but I have the ability to span space and time, our contract part of the equation. It is a beautiful thing we do, my love, and we are supported by so many higher dimensional beings. Great numbers of souls have come to this time in Earth's history with contracts of continued communication beyond the separation of realms: one in light body, one on the planet. It is part of the ascension process and humans awakening to the fact they are so much more than just body and form. There are many around the world who are doing death awareness work, the list of souls massive. We are helping to ease people into a new consciousness, a level of understanding of who they really are. Humans will all experience death of the 3D physical body, whether it is with someone they love or their own death journey. It is a threshold, one uniquely experienced by every individual. Each journey is heroic."

A Reiki training class I held in June was another adventure into healing energy and psychic insight. As part of the training, we go into guided meditations. I rested into meditation and, before I even visualized the forest path, Jack was there with butterflies swirling all around him. He smiled and thanked me for sharing our story of love in the book. (my chapter titled "Mayflies and Feathers" in the book *The Grateful Soul*, compiled by Kyra Schafer, As You Wish Publishing) He was telling me to remember the magic. Jack and I walked the familiar path through the forest as we laughed and joined arms. We sat at the log on the beach and discussed our current relationship and how we can stay connected. He grabbed my hand and led me out onto the ocean. The waves moved up and around me, swirling in orange and purple, engulfing me with incredible, healing flames. Then the ocean opened and I found myself in a large space, like a womb, the womb of Gaia. Jack backed away a bit and asked me to remember. I looked out and saw many souls crossing over, as well as angels and my family of light. Then I rested into being surrounded by and feeling the support of all those beings. Jack told me he is orchestrating things from his side to support our work together. He will be with me, supporting and assisting, as I write the book to come.

I was beginning to find comfort in my new life, which was starting to make sense. While I did not always like how our lives had played out, I found peace in seeing the bigger picture, understanding the information would be shared in a bigger way, part of the reason we came together. It was up to me to honor the sacrifice Jack had made so we could share this expanded way of experiencing life and death, heartache and love.

Jack reminded me, "There are many ways to stay connected. We did our own version of divine love, the Abler Soul. We contracted before we came to Earth to do this, my love, for us to explore the soul in this way. My leaving was necessary for both of us to evolve. You are understanding more and more the journey is expansive, full of many aspects of love, many freedoms. I am so free to be and expand in ways beyond my imagination and to be able to stay connected and infuse you with some of those same energies. Death is not to be feared. Yes, I know you miss me but again, just remember to breathe into me. The breath is a key while in the body. It is the mainline to Spirit and part of the physical form's ability to transmute energy while still embodied. Breath is alchemy. You alchemize energy with breath. I did not feel I could breathe into who I was while in physical form so I created scenarios to carry out our contract. It is all part of the web and often hard to fathom. You understand this, my love. Keep using your breath. Breathe into my freedom of spirit, my now existence. We share this wisdom together, working as one soul. We knew this at some level. Thank you for sharing the stories, my love. You honor me from your heart and I am so full of love and gratitude for your gift. I love you, Becki."

Remember the song Jack played for me before he passed? It was the one song he did not get recorded. I had been unable to pull the melody back into my conscious mind since that day. No matter how hard I tried to remember, it was gone, I thought lost. But on an early morning in June, I had a beautiful surprise. The song's beautiful melody was playing in my head, the one that touched my soul, and it was moving my consciousness awake. I felt Jack next to me and grabbed my pen and paper. I heard Jack say, "I am glad you heard me, my love. Thank you for listening. You are strong and needed to see you can be solid in your awareness. I am with you. Trust. Breathe into me! Synchronistic moments will keep showing you the way."

My fears about exposing myself to the judgment of others, of being vulnerable to scrutiny, of exposing myself and my love connection with Jack, were melting away and the pull to write the book Jack and I knew was coming, ever-present. We continue to fulfill our contract.

Jack's Message

Hello, my love. Breathe into me. Breathe me into you. You have done great. I have so much to share and yet the message simple. Our journey is one of love, complete sacrifice into the arms of the divine through the passage of death. But it was only the death of my form so the birth of my Spirit can be free to fulfill my expansion. I am so grateful you have given voice to my life and my eternal Spirit.

All who read, the writing of this book has been guided more than Becki realizes. The words flow in our channel but angels are all around the words, infusing them with an energy many will feel. The beauty of connection between humans and Spirit is a natural dance of energetic exchange. The higher humans ascend, the more they will feel the bond, the aliveness, the vibration of light. This type of connection to a soul, spirit, guide, light being, ascended master, will become commonplace, natural, part of the paradigm of an enlightened humanity.

My love, in the no-time we are always connected, always one blended essence in divine love. All you need to do is remember and breathe into me. I am here. We are not done; we have much more to share. Trust me, trust you, trust we. I love you.

The Expansion of Love Continues

"I never fully leave you because we are not separate, our souls one essence, blended into a dance of dimensional collapse, neither here nor completely there, but in a unique field of subtle oneness, a unity of divine love."

Jack, July 12

I would never tell you this journey has been easy, or that the pain of grief has not captured me in a stranglehold. Yet, with Spirit's help, I found the bravery to claw my way out. I will not discount how anyone feels after the losing a loved one, no matter the ethos of the relationship, but death need not be a slippery slope, a tabu subject, not discussed or avoided at all costs. We will transition out of this life, move into another beautiful realm of existence, and leave our loved ones behind. I am one example of a life found after loss, a life that makes sense to me. I work and commune with my beloved on the other side. When I step into the field of connection with him, my body is enlivened, I light up, and my soul remembers. I carry a luminescence I did not know was possible, because Jack helps me hold the torch.

We seldom give ourselves credit for the magnificent strength inside us. We can feel the emotions of sadness and smile at the joy of remembrance of an embrace. We are multi-dimensional beings, which means we can feel and experience it all in the same moment. Our fear is the limiting factor that keeps us imprisoned, fear we will be over-whelmed with heartbreak so strong we won't survive if we open the channels to intense emotion. Fear of emotion is our thinking-mind trying to keep us safe. Our mind does its job to help us swerve, avoid potholes in the road, take us on a detour. But the road ahead is where our higher awareness truly wants to go. We forget this: we have road workers ahead of us, our spiritual teams and loved ones, who fill those potholes so the emotional fallout does not damage us as much. We may still feel the bumps but it will be a little bit softer, a little bit easier ride, when we allow them to work alongside us.

Maybe I can help others fill in some of those potholes with the awareness I have gained along my journey's winding road. It brings me great joy to be in service to people who are finding they are letting go of life, entering the death passage, or, to those on the flip side, loss through the death of a loved one. We need not go through the death transition alone. No matter what the outside circumstances look like, we are never alone. There are people ready to assist, resources available for the finding but, most importantly, we are surrounded by beings of the higher realms, loved ones who have passed, angelic beings, our family of light, God. Please remember who you are, a light being or soul consciousness in a third-dimensional, temporary human form. As such, you have a direct line to Spirit connection if you so choose. It is your birthright.

Resources

Emily Beatrix, Intuitive Holistic Life Coach

Emily Beatrix Consulting *emilybeatrix.com*

Lee Harris, Intuitive Guide, Transformation Teacher, Musician

https://www.leeharrisenergy.com

Lorie Ladd, Ascension Teacher, Multidimensional Channel

http://lorieladd.com

Sherry Quarnstrom, Author, Intuitive Guide, Personal Empowerment Coach

www.Lifesculptingpathways.com

Maria Marathon, Heart Connection Coach and Musical Intuitive, Heart Song Activation Guide

Founder of Heart Song www.heartsong.se and https://heart-song.mykajabi.com/

HeartMath® Institute

https://www.heartmath.com

harps://www.heartmath.org

International Center for Reiki Training

https://www.reiki.org

National Hospice and Palliative Care Organization

https://www.nhpco.org

International End of Life Doula Association

https://www.inelda.org

Afterword

I am humbled by the outpouring of support for this book birthing into the world. The journey I wrote about is not for the faint of heart. This book is for the courageous, those willing to face life and death head-on. The number of people who are losing life, losing loved ones, is staggering. The baby boom generation is of age to transition but many of all ages are leaving.

My strength has been bolstered by the people I have met along the way who are searching for a new way to witness the death passage. Eartha and Steve are two such souls, Eartha still here and Steve, where Jack is in the realm of Spirit. We experienced similar loss but through different circumstances. Yet we share a common pull to the soul work Eartha, Steve, Jack, and I are here to fulfill. The more we met and explored life after our beloveds left, the more we recognized Jack and Steve share similar information, using slightly different language to explain the same concepts. We have been in awe of the magical connection to which we all contribute, the afterlife becoming tangible in our reality.

I asked Eartha to contribute her thoughts and ideas about the book. Our work together will evolve and I am honored to share the stage with these three incredible souls. Thank you, Eartha and Steve and Jack, my soul family. I know others of our soul family are out there and I anxiously await their introduction. Blessings to all who travel the death passage journey!

Eartha Love

Becki and I were guided to meet by our beloveds in Spirit, not long after my love Steve died in February 2020. We both assisted the transition of our partners from this Earth plane, and experienced a returning of our beloveds to us soon after their death. Through our hearts' broken openness and the ability to navigate the transition consciously, we have been awakened to the deep, ecstatic, Sacred union! Miracles and powerful synchronicities abound and we are held in love and trust. We have gone beyond the illusion of death into the realization that Soul stays alive, and some of us have chosen to be together across the veil, to fulfill a deeper Soul purpose and love across the dimensions, allowing our hearts and souls to become one. After all, truly, there is no separation.

It is not an easy path, to be with someone completely and utterly through their death process, never mind the love of your life! The pain of heartbreak is unbearable but Becki navigated it with grace and wisdom. She found the strength to see and witness Jack in his letting go, to deeply listen to the calling of his soul. Through surrendering herself, she switched on her soul Sat Nav, allowing her to be guided beyond her needs and wants, to feel the truth of the divine plan or soul contract between them. It was a courageous journey for both of them. As you read this book, I am sure you felt the courage, love, and strength it took to dive deep into their initiation.

Becki and Jack's story evokes tears that cleanse the windows of your soul's eyes and cracks open your heart to the path of remembering: the path of remembering we are love, we are Soul, and Spirit flows through us. We are part of the cosmos of living energy and we are Spirit having a human experience. When we awaken to these truths, we will bring heaven to Earth. This beauty-filled book will help that awakening, allowing us to see the world through our soul's eyes.

Eartha's Channeled Message with Steve

Becki and Jack's love and death story assist us all in feeling the sacredness of the death threshold and in feeling the holiness of the expansion it brings. Their story helps us have reverence for this sacred passage, whether we are moving through our physical death or rites of passage threshold.

Death is the ultimate sacrifice for love, for the continuation of life. It is nothing to fear. It is another beginning, a rebirth, a birth. Sacrifice is required to be able to resurrect oneself into the unfolding new life.

Death in its unfolding is the loving expression of universal love, because we become the one heart, one soul, that surrounds and is everything: consciousness, the aliveness, the life force. To resist death goes against the tide of love that washes us clean, clean from heavy, dense energy, that which has no life force. The new is the rebirth, the renewal required for life to continue. To resist death is to create suffering and density on this Earth plane.

Death is an expansion. The one heart, one love that is death consciousness seeks to know itself in this life. It is a constant motion toward Soul, a continuation and unfolding.

At this time on Earth, our soul family is assisting humanity in moving beyond the illusion of death and into the reality of the love this will bring to the Earth plane. Becki and Jack are part of our soul family who are assisting in this process. The bringing of their message through this book to the world is for the beginning of a new way on this planet, a new way that will see people come back together in love as they remember their soul. The love present during Jack's death process enabled the consciousness that is Jack to exit without fear and to evolve as a light being. In turn, his evolving consciousness affects Becki's soul. She is able to begin to navigate Earth's shifts in a way that brings trust and love in the process. Many departed souls are making a choice to stay connected to their loved ones after death.

It was and is Jack and Becki's intense soul love that enabled the creation of the Abler Soul. We are helping to seed love in the world through our soul purpose. Their book is one such seed.

Through conscious death, we realize love is the part of life that exists outside of the confines of the mind; it is the thing of which we are all made, everything. The death process starts with a huge letting go and surrender of oneself and then an opening, opening to the magnificent radiance and light which is permeated with love. We begin to feel this light, this love, the more we let go of the need, wants, and desires that come from a place of fear, holding on, and codependency. There is nothing more beautiful than love coming from the openness and surrender to all that is, to life unfolding, to life becoming, to life as it is and as it expresses itself through us.

Love exists everywhere; it is the basic component of the universe.

Our soul is love, just as Consciousness is love.

Through conscious death, we are awakened to the fifth-dimension reality and phase of renewal being birthed in the world. Nothing stays the same in the universe; all is evolving, even Consciousness.

Many souls are doing different things in the universe and it all works together as one. It is all one. There is Becki's soul essence expressing itself and Jack's, and their Abler Soul has merged with the eternal.

The path of soul love is a form of spiritual practice transcending death and welcoming evolutionary ways of consciousness manifesting on Earth and beyond. Even heaven is an old concept. Everything is in flux. It is fed by consciousness on the Earth plane, which is fed by consciousness on the 5D plane, and it evolves together, merging. That is why the work is seeding love, bringing 5D down to 3D, transforming the world and opening the path of the heart in remembering and staying alive after death.

To hold on through fear is to the detriment of oneself, soul, life, and love.

There truly is nothing to fear; there is only love.

Through reading this book we hope all can learn to grieve well, dive deep, awaken to Soul, and then find our way to celebrate this unfolding life in all its holiness.

This book, their love story, shows us the light inside the dark, that love is truly stronger than death, and how we can truly live the Sacred, love one another, and realize our divinity.

Eartha and Sunheart 2020

Eartha Love, Restoring Community, Rites of Passage, Culture and the Land

Author of the upcoming book "Soul Mending, Rites of Passage For a Changing World"

www. *sacredwomansacredworld.org*

www. *womanbecoming.org*

Acknowledgments

My gratitude for my life is immeasurable, an energetic experience that fills my being with love and light. Many people have contributed to my healing and assisted in writing this book that I now share.

Above all else, I want to honor my co-author, my beloved Jack. A part of me so wishes this book did not exist, that the book I was to write would be on another topic; but here we are, writing in tandem, together, I in the physical and he in the realm of Spirit. I cannot think of any greater service in my life than to share our love with others through written words we write hand-in-hand as one soul.

I could not have navigated this death passage without my family's comfort; my mom Kathleen, my dad Lionel, who joined us from Spirit, my son TJ, my daughter Brandee and son-in-law Nate, my granddaughters, Ada and Clara. They were not only present during Jack's transition but were the salve to my open wound afterward, calming the pain with their love and light. I also want to thank my brother Tony and his family and my sister Nicole and her family for their energetic embrace holding me from a distance, feeding love into my soul, along with the rest of my extended family. I want to thank my landlords Jay and Donna, who are like family to Jack and me. In his spirit form, Jay often visits Donna and me and I am forever grateful for their kind support.

Many family and friends lent energetic solace and financial assistance during and after, and while too many to name, there are a few key people who I feel called to mention; Jozy, Adele, Mike, Susan, Sherry, Maria, Paul, Bill, Nick, Mercedes, Charles, Sonja, Keely, Kellie, Jeanie, Peggy, Heidi, Inge, Diana, Terry, Jane, Eve, Megan, Saira, and Kris, thank you.

I am honored to have a fantastic team of Energy Intuitives who have mentored me along the way; had an enormous impact on my journey of awakening into new levels of awareness and expansion of soul expression. Thank you, Lee Harris, Lorie Ladd, Emily Beatrix, and Sherry Quarnstrom, for your loving and gentle guidance into the realms of spiritual self-empowerment.

Praise for this book has come in many forms. I appreciate all who have taken the time to read through the draft manuscript. Adele Lewis, author and friend, has been by my side for many years and has made this book much better for her editing skills. She has a Reiki-for-life golden ticket. Jane Berryhill, author, friend, and business partner, lent her expertise to the manuscript, and we are having a lot of fun creating video content and new business ventures together. Both women also wrote a paragraph of praise for the book. My friend of many years who walks this death passage walk with me, Terry Du Beau, shared words as did dear friends and soul sisters Maria Marathon and Sherry Quarnstrom. Ladies, you rock my world!

Acknowledgments

Christina Oss LaBang was kind enough to share her thoughts and experience in the Forward from the perspective of a seasoned Hospice RN and author of her beautiful book, *ANDEANsolrocks: Pathway of Light*. I carry her books in my business, Step Stone, and have used the stones regularly since finding them. They are a gift that resonates with my soul and the stones, well, they vibrate in my hands. Need I say more? Thank you, Christina, in so many ways.

I warmly acknowledge my clients. Your continued belief in me and my work has helped me have the confidence to step forward, shine my light, and let go of self-judgment and fear. Your experiences have continually inspired me and held me up when I felt the waves of grief wash over me.

Eartha and Steve, it is hard to put into words the depth of my gratitude for our shared journey. My heart aches with you for your personal physical loss, and my heart is elated for you in the blissful joy of divine connection. It is a strange dichotomy we share and yet one that will continue to grow in size as we meet others who are experiencing similar relationships with loved ones from beyond the veil. I look forward to our continued expansion and work in the world. Thank you for being my soul family.

I want to thank Kyra and Todd Schafer of As You Wish Publishing. Your course, *Build Your Brilliant Book*, lit a fire in my soul, and this book is the result. You are an exceptional team for the independent writer, and your self-publishing options are helping us get our messages out into the world. Your vision is excellent, and your hearts even greater. Thank you for your guidance and support along the way. I am honored to be among the cadre of authors at As You Wish Publishing.

I know there are those not explicitly mentioned but who have impacted the writing of this book. I thank you. I appreciate all the people, souls, angels, and light beings cheering this book on.

My love goes out to the readers who braved the profound emotional challenge this book asked of you; I understand the intense energy in these pages. Jack made it clear that readers, if open to the possibilities, would experience a transference, a catalytic opportunity for healing and connection. I thank you from the bottom of my heart for participating and honoring our life, your life, and the life of others. The journey of death can be seen as an expansion by those who are open. Even though I may not know all of the readers, I know them through Soul, the divine heart connection I saw in my beautiful vision. We are not separate.

Finally, in complete surrender, I acknowledge the Higher Awareness expressed as Becki. The writing of Jack's and my journey took a willingness to be open and a vulnerability I am not sure I would have reached without the unwavering divine essence I feel moving through me. Sometimes our journeys are beyond our limited 3D comprehension, but when we move into faith in a higher purpose, a connection to a higher light, we can let go of resistance and realize we are all a gift in human form on planet Earth. We each have a story to share that will help someone else. Even if all we do is hold our light, stand within our divine human nature, we are enough.

About The Author

Becki Koon is a Heart-based Energy Intuitive, Holy Fire III®
Reiki Master, HeartMath® Coach, Life Coach, Crystal
Practitioner, and Author/Speaker. Through her business,
Step Stone, Becki empowers people to seek their inner
wisdom while holding space for them to heal, discover, and
grow into the next highest version of themselves. She likes
to refer to herself as the mid-wife of birthing a person's
remembrance of their divine essence or soul purpose.

Becki's work has recently evolved in a way she never
expected. When her husband of 12 years passed, she knew
her life was forever changed. She did not expect that she
would wake up to the capability of communication with him
through spirit mediumship. Now, in Reiki and other healing
sessions, Becki receives guidance from not only Jack but her
angelic guides and family of light, other people's guides,
loved ones who have passed, and ascended masters. The
world of channeling higher beings is a gift she says is a salve
that has helped her deal with loss and grief. Being in service
to others through sharing the process of conscious death has
given her an outlet for the compassionate wisdom gained.
Their process of experiencing conscious death together has
changed her life, her work, her very essence, and she vows
to continue using the gifts he so lovingly encouraged her to
remember and offer to the world. The transition from the
physical body to soul essence need not be frightening but can
be a beautiful honoring and celebration of LIFE and LOVE
never-ending.

Contact:

stepstone2you@gmail.com

www.beckikoon.com

www.facebook.com/becki.koon.consulting

www.amazon.com/author/beckikoon